SRA ART Connections

Artist Profiles

SRA
Columbus, OH

The McGraw·Hill Companies

Photo Credits

3 Courtesy of Abrasha; 4 Courtesy of the Arthur M. Sackler Museum, Harvard University Art Museums, Gift of John Goelet, Formerly in the Collection of Louis J. Cartier. Photo ©2003 President and Fellows of Harvard College; 5 ©Bettmann/Corbis; 6 ©Arthur Rothstein/Corbis; 7 ©1975 Helaine Victoria Press; 8 Courtesy of Jonathan Borofsky; 9 ©Private Collection/The Bridgeman Art Library; 10 ©Getty Images; 11 ©The Western Reserve Historical Society, Cleveland, Ohio; 12 Courtesy of Robert Cottingham/Forum Gallery; 13 Courtesy of Bing Davis. Photo by Melvin Greer; 14 ©Norman Parkinson Limited/Fiona Cowan/Corbis; 15 ©Francis G. Mayer/Corbis; 16 Courtesy of Aboriginal Fine Arts Gallery; 17 ©John Gruen courtesy Marlborough Gallery; 18 ©Oscar White/Corbis; 19 ©Ann Chwatsky; 20 Art Museum Miami University, Oxford, Ohio; 21 International Folk Art Foundation Collection, Museum of International Folk Art. Santa Fe, New Mexico. Photo by: Michel Monteaux; 22 ©Getty Images; 23 ©Christopher Felver/Corbis; 24 Courtesy of John Hoover; 25 ©National Portrait Gallery, Smithsonian Institution/Art Resource, NY; 26 ©Albert Casciero; 27 Courtesy, Toh-Atin Gallery; 28 Photo by Willis Bing Davis; 29 ©Peter Bolenheu; 30 ©Archiv/Interfoto; 31 ©Culver Pictures; 32 Courtesy of Ole Lundin; 33 ©Black Images; 34 ©Eric Schaal/Getty Images; 35 ©McMichael Canadian Art Collection Archives, Gift of Marjorie Lismer Bridges; 36 Courtesy of Jeff Miller/UW-Madison University Communications, 2002; 37 ©Photothèque R. Magritte-ADAGP / Art Resource, NY; 38 Courtesy of Alexander and Bonin, NY. Photo by Peter Bellamy; 39 ©UPI/Corbis-Bettmann; 40 ©Hiroshi Okuda; 41 ©Archive Photos; 42 Courtesy of Philip Moulthrop; 43 ©Bettmann/Corbis; 44 ©Getty Images; 45 ©Bettmann/Corbis; 46 ©1945 Arnold Newman; 47 ©Corbis; 48 Sid Richardson Collection of Western Art, Fort Worth, Texas; 49 Photo by C'Love; 50 Library of Congress/Corbis; 51 ©Art Resource, NY; 52 Courtesy John P. Russell/Photograph by Herbert Bauer; 53 The National Museum of Women in the Arts, Washington, DC. Gift of Wallace and Wilhelmina Holladay; 54 ©Timothy Greenfield-Sanders; 55 ©Michael Nicholson/Corbis; 56 Courtesy of Ann Vytlacil Williams; 57 ©Hulton/Getty Images; 58 Courtesy Schmidt-Bingham Gallery. Photo by Joe De Rosa; 59 Jock McDonald; 60 Copyright ©1996, The Heard Museum (Phoenix, AZ)/Photo by Tamea Mikesell; 61 Dallas Museum of Art; 62 Birmingham Museum of Art Birmingham, Gift of Ruby McAllister; 63 The Metropolitan Museum of Art, Gift of Mrs. Edward S. Harkness, 1916. (16.99). Photograph ©1983 The Metropolitan Museum of Art; 64 The Asia Society, New York, Mr. and Mrs. John D. Rockefeller III Collection/Photo by Lynton Gardiner; 65 Detroit Institute of Arts, Detroit, Michigan; 66 The Metropolitan Museum of Art, Gift of Mrs. J. Insley Blair, 1950. Photograph ©1981 The Metropolitan Museum of Art; 67 The Seattle Art Museum, Gift of Jack Lenor Larson. Photo by Paul Macapia; 68 The Metropolitan Museum of Art, Fletcher Fund, 1934 (34.33) Photograph ©1995 The Metropolitan Museum of Art; 69 The Asia Society, New York, Mr. and Mrs. John D. Rockefeller III Collection/Photo by Lynton Gardiner; 70 The Metropolitan Museum of Art, The Harry G.C. Packard Collection of Asian Art, Gift of Harry G. C. Packard and Purchase, Fletcher, Rogers, Harris Brisbane Dick and Louis V. Bell Funds, Joseph Pulitzer Bequest and The Annenberg Fund, Inc. Gift, 1975 (1975.268.182). Photograph ©1983 The Metropolitan Museum of Art; 71 Dallas Museum of Art. Dallas, Texas; 72 The Metropolitan Museum of Art, Harris Brisbane Dick Fund, 1939. (39.20) Photograph ©1982 The Metropolitan Museum of Art; 74 Museum of Fine Arts, Houston; 75 The Metropolitan Museum of Art, Gift of Edward S. Harkness, 1918. Photograph ©1979 The Metropolitan Museum of Art; 76 Kimbell Art Museum; 77 The Metropolitan Museum of Art, the Michael C. Rockefeller Collection, Purchase, Nelson A. Rockefeller Gift, 1964. (1978.412.489) Photograph by Schecter Lee. Photograph © 1986 The Metropolitan Museum of Art; 78 The Metropolitan Museum of Art, The Michael C. Rockefeller Memorial Collection, Bequest of Nelson A. Rockefeller, 1979. (1979.206.1131) Photograph ©1981 The Metropolitan Museum of Art; 79 ©Ron Watts/Corbis; 80 Smithsonian National Museum of the American Indian, New York; 81 From the Girard Foundation Collection, in the Museum of International Folk Art, a unit of the Museum of New Mexico, Santa Fe, New Mexico; 82 The Metropolitan Museum of Art. New York; 83 Smithsonian American Art Museum/Art Resource, NY.

SRAonline.com

McGraw Hill SRA

Copyright © 2005 by SRA/McGraw-Hill.

All rights reserved. Except as permitted under the United States Copyright Act, no part of this publication may be reproduced or distributed in any form or by any means, or stored in a database or retrieval system, without the prior written permission of the publisher, unless otherwise indicated.

Send all inquiries to:
SRA/McGraw-Hill
4400 Easton Commons
Columbus, OH 43219

Printed in the United States of America.

ISBN 0-07-601836-9

2 3 4 5 6 7 8 9 DBH 08 07

Table of Contents

Abrasha 3
Áli, Mir Sayyid 4
Audubon, John James 5
Avery, Milton 6
Bonheur, Rosa 7
Borofsky, Jonathan 8
Caillebotte, Gustave 9
Canaletto 10
Cole, Allen E. 11
Cottingham, Robert 12
Davis, Willis "Bing" 13
de Saint Phalle, Niki 14
Degas, Edgar 15
Djukulul, Dorothy 16
Estes, Richard 17
Evergood, Philip 18
Fish, Janet 19
Flack, Audrey 20
Flores, Aurelio and Francisco 21
Gainsborough, Thomas 22
Held, Al 23
Hoover, John 24
Hopper, Edward 25
Jean-Gilles, Joseph 26
John, Isabel 27
Jones, Calvin 28
Kabotie, Fred 29
Kandinsky, Wassily 30
Klee, Paul 31
Kudo, Lundin 32
Lawrence, Jacob 33
Leger, Fernand 34
Lismer, Arthur 35
Loeser, Tom 36
Magritte, René 37
Mangold, Sylvia Plimack 38
Matisse, Henri 39
Miyawaki, Ayako 40
Monet, Claude 41
Moulthrop, Philip 42

Nevelson, Louise 43
O'Keeffe, Georgia 44
Picasso, Pablo 45
Pippin, Horace 46
Ray, Man 47
Remington, Fredric 48
Ringgold, Faith 49
Rivera, Diego 50
Rousseau, Henri 51
Russell, Shirley 52
Spitzmueller, Pamela 53
Thiebaud, Wayne 54
Turner, Joseph 55
Vytlacil, Vaclav 56
Warhol, Andy 57
Weber, Idelle 58
Wiley, William 59
Youngblood, Nancy 60
Child's Beaded Shirt 61
Collar 62
Cover of an Armenian book 63
Covered Jar 64
Double Saddlebag 65
Easy Chair 66
Hat: Birds and Geometric Patterns 67
Hunting Scene on Handle from a Large Bowl 68
Jar 69
Jar 70
Mask with Seal or Sea Otter Spirit 71
Mihrab 72
Necklace 73
Necklace 74
Portrait of a Boy 75
Presentation of Captives to a Maya Ruler 76
Senufo Face Mask 77
Sleeveless Shirt 78
Symmetrical View of a Totem Pole 79
Thunderbird Shield 80
Tree of Life 81
Tunic 82
Washington's Headquarters 83
Window, Hairdresser's (John Sloan) 84

Artist Profile

Abrasha
b. 1948

The goldsmith and jewelry designer Abrasha (ə brä´ shə), who uses his first name only, was born in Holland in 1948. After apprenticing as a goldsmith for years in Europe, he immigrated to the United States in 1977. Soon after his arrival in America, Abrasha began teaching jewelry making at art schools in the San Francisco Bay area. In the many years he has lived in the Bay area, he has taught, lectured, created and exhibited artwork, and collaborated with other artists. Abrasha's work is exhibited in museums and galleries throughout the country. He is a member of the Society of North American Goldsmiths and has received numerous honors and awards in the United States and Germany.

About Art History

Abrasha created this simple, beautiful Hanukkah menorah in memory of his father, Solomon David Staszewski, who was a survivor of the Holocaust. Staszewski had been imprisoned in a death camp that was a satellite of Auschwitz. Abrasha began creating more serious works after participating in therapy groups for the children of Holocaust survivors. He creates these meaningful pieces as a way to feel connected to his Jewish heritage.

About the Artwork

Abrasha created the Hanukkah menorah in response to an invitation to participate in the Jewish Museum of San Francisco's Hanukkah Menorah Invitational. As he began to plan and design the Hanukkah menorah, Abrasha followed the original *Shulchan Aruch,* the Jewish code of law, for the requirements of a proper Hanukkah menorah. He used the traditional materials and proportions for this special type of menorah when creating the piece. Although it is a magnificent original artwork, this Hanukkah menorah was also designed and constructed to be functional.

About the Media

This Hanukkah menorah is made of stainless steel, sterling silver, and 24-karat gold. The steel cups at the top of the menorah hold olive oil, which burns when a wick in each cup is set alight.

About the Technique

Abrasha consulted and followed the dictates of the *Shulchan Aruch* as he made his Hanukkah menorah. The materials he used to construct the menorah, the spacing of the lights, and the type of oil used for lighting the cups all conformed to the Jewish code of law.

▲ **Mir Sayid Áli.** (Persian).
Nighttime in a Palace. c. 1539–1543.

Opaque watercolor, gold, and silver on paper. 11.26 × 7.87 inches (28.6 × 20 cm.). Arthur M. Sackler Museum, Harvard University, Cambridge, Massachussetts.

• Artist Profile •

Mir Sayyid Áli

Mir Sayyid Ali (mēr sä´yēd äl´ē) was one of the great masters of Iranian Mughal painting during the Safavid dynasty. The Safavid dynasty, between 1499 and 1722 A.D., saw the production of some of the most ornate and exquisite mural paintings, ink drawings, illustrations, and portraits in history. Mughal art is an Indo-Islamic-Persian style of painting and architecture that originated in and around India and Pakistan during the Mughal Empire. During the time that *Nighttime in a Palace* was created, Mir Sayyid Ali worked in the imperial studio of Shah Tahmasp I, a notable Safavid patron of the arts. In 1549, Mir Sayyid Ali left the Safavid court and began to work for the Mughal emperor Humayun, who was in exile in Kabul. In 1555, when Humayun reconquered India, Mir Sayyid Ali followed the emperor and was rewarded with the position of master of the newly formed Mughal court workshop.

About Art History

The miniature was one type of artwork popular in Persia during the time period when *Nighttime in a Palace* was created. Persian artists depicted candid scenes from everyday life in these tiny, incredibly detailed miniature paintings. The movements and expressions of the characters in different scenes tell a story and allow viewers to glimpse a moment of time in sixteenth-century Persia.

About the Artwork

Nighttime in a Palace is a watercolor miniature that depicts a lively scene from the court of the Bihzad Palace of the Safavid dynasty, which was located in what is today the country of Iran. This colorful painting is full of animated characters, beautiful architecture, and amazingly intricate details. The artist used fine details to bring his characters to life and to tell different stories from each level and location within the palace: musicians entertain a Sultan; merchants sell their wares; servants wait on nobility; a youth dances; furtive ladies watch the festivities; and children sit atop the palace roof. The painting succeeds in showing the energy and flurry of activity of Bihzid Palace nightlife.

About the Media

Nighttime in a Palace was created with watercolors and gold leaf on paper. The work is a miniature, measuring only 28.6 centimeters by 20 centimeters.

About the Technique

Mir Sayyid Ali focused his attention on the actions of the characters in this painting, adding colorful details to each individual. The palace is painted with an absence of depth and shadows, suggesting that the building is simply a backdrop for the activities of the people within.

Artist Profile

John James Audubon
1785–1851

John James Audubon (jän jāmz ô´ də bən) was born in Santo Domingo, now Haiti. His mother died a few months after he was born, so he was raised in France by his father and his father's wife, a kind woman who encouraged his love of the outdoors and art. When he was 18, he left France for America to live on one of his father's plantations in Pennsylvania. Audubon drew birds only as a hobby until he and his family met with hard financial times. Audubon's successful journeys established him as a leading romantic painter and expert on ornithology. Years after his death the National Audubon Society was founded in his name.

About Art History

At age 18, Audubon arrived in Pennsylvania to live on his father's estate and escape conscription into Napoleon's army. He had a comfortable business career until 1819, when he was briefly jailed for bankruptcy and forced to seek prospects elsewhere. Sailing down the Mississippi, the artist led a rugged life documenting and painting studies of birds. In 1826, he sailed to England with his collection *Birds of America*. His paintings were an immediate success, and he was given free painting lessons by the portrait artist Thomas Sully, who encouraged his efforts. In 1843, Audubon made his last trip west to create his final series of paintings, *Viviparous Quadrupeds of North America,* a study of mammals.

About the Artwork

Each life-sized, highly embellished bird portrait was depicted in great detail and accompanied by Audubon's descriptions and observations of wildlife. He would spend weeks painting day and night on some of his compositions, painstakingly rendering each feather or nuance of form. In *Carolina Parakeet,* Audubon displayed the now extinct bird in numerous postures and drew attention to its rapidly dwindling population. At the time, Carolina parakeets were hunted for their feathers and regarded as pests, and farmers would shoot them by the thousands. This print is considered one of Audubon's most exceptional pieces.

About the Media

Audubon drew and painted using a combination of watercolors, graphite, gouache, crayon, and pastel on selectively glazed paper. He also painted some of his compositions in oils.

About the Technique

Audubon began drawing in the fields and forests of his home merely for recreation and enjoyment. As his career progressed he went on numerous expeditions around the country, climbing mountains and trees, and fording swamps and rivers, to obtain views of his subjects. Audubon studied a bird in its natural habitat and sketched it many times before beginning a final print.

Artist Profile

Milton Avery
1893–1965

Milton Avery (mil´ tən ā´ və rē) was born in New York but grew up in Connecticut. He loved to paint and travel, and he also loved nature, landscapes, and color. Around 1905, Avery attended both the Connecticut League of Art Students in Hartford, Connecticut, and later the School of the Art Society in Hartford. Often he would paint all day long in his New York studio, sometimes creating five or six paintings or studies in a day. He established himself as a dedicated color field painter. He spent 50 years of his life painting, and created thousands of works of art.

About Art History

In 1925, after encountering the work of Matisse and Picasso, Avery began to simplify and abstract his own painting, although he never lost focus of representational subject matter. By the 1940s, he had eliminated almost all painted detail and was utilizing patterns of flattened shapes and arbitrary colors like Matisse. Avery's emphasis on color strongly influenced the work of younger artists, such as Rothko, Frankenthaler, Gottlieb, and Newman, who were called color field painters. Avery was also a good friend of another American modernist, Hartley.

About the Artwork

Avery's paintings were said to combine modernism with folk art, a unique style for his time. By painting abstractly, Avery's use of color played an even larger role in his work, for it was expressive and suggested a subject. His use of color fields determined his portrayal of space and form, as in the painting *Mountain and Meadow*, where the spaces between simple mountains are created by a change in color.

About the Media

Most of Avery's numerous paintings were completed using oil on canvas. Because he generated so many paintings so swiftly, his sketches were usually outlined directly onto his canvases, although he did study figure drawing for a long time in art school.

About the Technique

Color field painters filled vast sections of their canvases with fields of color, sometimes using only a few hues to designate space or form. Avery applied his paint in large sections, simplifying the form of his subjects and using wide brushes to fill the canvas. For many of his paintings, he applied paint rapidly, which allowed him to experiment and create numerous paintings at one time.

Artist Profile

Rosa Bonheur
1822–1899

Rosa Bonheur (rō´ za bä nur´) was a French painter and sculptor of the nineteenth century. She learned to paint from her artist father and from studying art in museums. Bonheur showed her works regularly at the Paris Salon, the principal exhibition space in France, where she won many awards. She later exhibited her art in England, where it was also very popular. She was the first female to be made an officer of the Legion of Honor—a recognition of accomplishment from the French government. As a female artist of the nineteenth century, Bonheur faced many restrictions. For example, she had to obtain a police permit to wear trousers while painting animals at a slaughterhouse.

About Art History

Bonheur probably did not witness many of the scenes she painted, but used her individual studies of landscape and animals to create her artwork.

About the Artwork

Bonheur is known for the naturalistic manner in which she painted and sculpted images of animals. She also painted everyday scenes and events based on her observations of nature.

About the Media

Bonheur painted with oils on canvas. Oil paint is created by mixing dry pigments into an oil base. The oil was painted on a canvas of heavy, woven fabric.

About the Technique

Bonheur used oil on canvas to create a thick, textured surface. This technique slows down the drying process, allowing the artist more time to include detail.

Artist Profile

Jonathan Borofsky
b. 1942

Jonathan Borofsky (jon´ a thən bor´ of skē) was born in Boston, Massachusetts. His mother, a painter of still lifes, encouraged him to take private painting lessons from the time he was eight until he graduated from high school. He studied art at Carnegie Mellon University in Pittsburgh and went on to study figure modeling at the École de Fontainebleau in Paris, France. He received his graduate degree from Yale School of Art and Architecture in 1966. Borofsky lived in New York City and Los Angeles for several years, eventually moving to Maine in 1992.

Borofsky gave up creating objects for a few years beginning in 1967, and began writing numbers on paper. When he returned to actively creating works of art, he began signing his work with the number he had reached at each piece's completion.

About Art History

When Borofsky began working in the 1960s and 1970s, *minimalism,* in which art is reduced to the minimal number of elements, and *conceptualism,* in which art conveys a concept or idea, were important styles of art. The influence of minimalism can be seen in his simple works, although unlike minimalists, Borofsky wishes to communicate an idea through his artwork.

About the Artwork

Borofsky created sculptural objects in his early years. By the 1960s he began experimenting with conceptual art and worked on thinking and writing exercises as well as drawings, paintings, and sculptures. He has also created wall paintings. Many of his exhibitions and installations were created on site at galleries and museums. Borofsky is interested in the subject of time; he once said, "My goal is to present . . . illustrations of my thoughts regarding the meaning of time."

About the Media

Borofsky works in many different media, including ink, acrylic paints, enamel, charcoal, aluminum, and found objects. He has created environmental installations in museums and galleries.

About the Technique

Borofsky often begins by creating a drawing that flows freely from his mind. He takes this image and finds new ways to use it, such as drawing larger versions of it or turning it into a sculpture or wall painting.

Gustave Caillebotte. (French).
Self Portrait with Pith Helmet. Nineteenth century.

Oil on canvas.
Private Collection/Bridgeman Art Library

Artist Profile

Gustave Caillebotte
1848–1894

Gustave Caillebotte (gūs´ täv kī´ yə bôt´) was born into a wealthy Parisian family. He earned a degree in law and was drafted into the French army. After serving in the Franco-Prussian War, he started painting. He was accepted into Paris's École des Beaux-Arts, but he decided against formal training. Caillebotte was attracted to the artistic rebels of the time, the impressionists. When the Impressionists began to disagree and the group broke up, Caillebotte moved from Paris to a French village. He continued to paint until his death, and he left his large collection of art to several museums.

About Art History

After painting in a French realist style, Caillebotte began to use light and shadow in an impressionistic way. In 1874, Edgar Degas invited Caillebotte to participate in an impressionist exhibition. By 1876, Caillebotte had joined the group, and was deeply influenced by his friends, Degas, Renoir, and Monet. He had inherited a large sum of money from his family and helped support other impressionists by buying their work.

About the Artwork

Early in his career, Caillebotte painted scenes of working-class life in Paris and portraits of his family and friends. Gradually he became more interested in the angles and architecture in his scenes than in the people he was painting. After he left Paris he painted landscapes of the Seine River, the Normandy countryside, seaside villas, and his personal garden and greenhouse.

About the Media

Caillebotte worked mainly in oils.

About the Technique

Toward the end of his brief career, Caillebotte used the broken brushwork of the impressionists. Along with capturing a single moment, he also emphasized interesting angles in his paintings. He painted his subjects from different perspectives—from above, from behind, with their backs to the light, or framed in a window.

Artist Profile

Canaletto
1697–1768

Giovanni Antonio Canal, known as Canaletto (ka na´ lāt tō), was born in Venice, Italy. He first began to paint with his father, who was a painter of theatre scenery. Canaletto traveled to Rome in 1719 and may have studied with painters of classical ruins. He began to paint dramatic city views of festivals and ceremonies for which he became very famous. Travelers from England often bought his paintings as souvenirs of their trips. Canaletto eventually moved to England and painted there for ten years. He then returned to Venice and continued to work for the remainder of his life.

About Art History

Italian art had become less important by the 1700s—the best art of the time came from countries such as Holland and France—but many talented artists continued to live in Venice. The most famous type of Venetian artist was the *veduta,* or "view-painter," and Canaletto was the most famous veduta of the eighteenth century. His views were painted using the *rococo* style, which focused on the carefree life of the wealthy rather than on historical or religious subjects.

About the Artwork

Canaletto's earliest paintings of Venice were unusual because he painted them while looking at the city—most artists at the time worked from drawings. He is most famous for painting views of Venice that accurately reflected different parts of the city. During his stay in England, Canaletto painted scenes of the English countryside. Later, he began to create more fantastic paintings. Work from the later years of his life has been criticized as being somewhat lifeless and dull.

About the Media

Canaletto generally used oil paints on stretched canvases.

About the Technique

Canaletto typically used delicate colors in his paintings. As he developed his style, his lines became more firm and detailed, and emphasized the accuracy of his paintings. Canaletto often used a camera obscura when preparing to paint. A *camera obscura* is a closed box with a lens and a mirror; the lens focuses an image, such as a scene of Venice, onto a panel so the artist can trace the image.

Artist Profile

Allen E. Cole
1884–1970

Allen Cole (al´ ən kōl) was an American photographer known for his pictures of people and places during the Great Depression. Cole did not plan to be a photographer. After high school and college he worked as a railroad porter, a real estate developer, and a waiter. After being injured in a train accident, Cole met Joseph Opet, a studio manager in Cleveland, Ohio, who introduced him to photography. He opened his first studio in his home in 1922.

About Art History

Cole's pictures of Cleveland during the 1930s are sometimes compared to those of James Van der Zee, who photographed Harlem in New York City during the 1960s. Cole's photographs, like Van der Zee's, invite viewers to better understand a particular group of people and the stressful time in which they lived.

About the Artwork

Cole's work shows the richness and variety of African American life in Cleveland during the Great Depression. He photographed groups and individuals, creating 30,000 negatives and 6,000 prints during his lifetime. His pictures offer glimpses of African American social, cultural, business, and religious groups that struggled and often succeeded during the Depression.

About the Media

Cole produced black-and-white photographs.

About the Technique

Cole did not snap informal pictures. Instead he carefully posed people to get the best visual effect. He included details in each photograph to help viewers understand the lives of the subjects. For example, a photograph he took in 1935 shows young newsboys gathered around a shiny bicycle. The photograph suggests that a bicycle was the center of these boys' lives because it helped them make a living. However, it is clear that their bikes were rarely as shiny and new as the one in the picture.

Artist Profile

Robert Cottingham
b. 1935

Neon signs, storefronts, and shop awnings are only a few of the many subjects Robert Cottingham (räb´ ərt côt´ ting hem) uses in his photorealistic artwork. Born in Brooklyn, New York, Cottingham grew up with an appreciation for the urban environment. He studied art at the Pratt Institute and worked as an art director for advertising companies in New York and Los Angeles. In 1968, he quit his job to become a full-time artist and began painting the buildings of Los Angeles. As he worked, he began to look higher and higher and realized that there was a world of familiar commercial imagery right above his head. This realization led to Cottingham's successful career as a photorealist and continues to emerge in his work today.

About Art History

When he moved to Los Angeles, Cottingham focused on the pop culture of Hollywood and the urban iconography of dilapidated downtown areas. He had his first exhibition in New York in 1971 and quickly became associated with the photorealism movement that included other artists such as Richard Estes and Chuck Close. He began printmaking in the early 1970s when he and several other photorealistic artists were invited to make an edition of prints.

About the Artwork

Cottingham is a *photorealist,* which means that his work is as detailed and realistic as a photograph. Cottingham thinks his work is successful if it can be viewed as both a realistic depiction and a formal painting, or a work that relies solely on the shape and form of its subject. Sometimes Cottingham recycles his images, using subject matter from a print in later paintings or a painted image in a print series. *Jane's Remington* portrays a typewriter on a slight angle and every detail is painted, which causes viewers to wonder if it is or is not a photograph.

About the Media

Cottingham is a painter and printmaker who uses oil and acrylic paint, as well as a variety of printmaking techniques including woodcuts, linoleum cuts, etching, and lithography. Many of the photos he has taken for his paintings are of the areas around bus terminals. He has traveled by Greyhound bus around the country to take photos.

About the Technique

Cottingham uses his camera as a sketchbook, taking photos as references and developing them into slides. He draws a grid on paper and projects the photographic image onto this grid. He then creates a black and white drawing from this projection. Next he creates one or more color studies in gouache or watercolor. When he is satisfied with the color study, Cottingham transfers either the original slide or the reworked drawing onto the canvas by projection or by grids.

Artist Profile

Willis "Bing" Davis
b. 1937

Bing Davis (bing dā´ vəs) was born in Dayton, Ohio. He was a student with many talents and gifts, including those for athletics and the arts. Because he excelled in sports, he was awarded a scholarship to DePauw University in Indiana, where he earned a degree in art education. He continued to study and earned his master's degree from Miami University in Oxford, Ohio. Davis has pioneered such projects as the Dayton-based, now nationwide, program Artists in the Schools. Davis has had more than 50 one-man exhibitions since 1959.

About Art History
Davis's style is a combination of African and African American styles. A fellowship to the country of Nigeria led him to explore the customs and heritage of his ancestors. This understanding of where he comes from spiritually and ethnically is incorporated into his artwork.

About the Artwork
Davis's artwork pays tribute to his African heritage. He transfers his ideas from one medium to the next. For example, he approaches much of his work in clay in the same way as he does collage, working with similar patterns and themes. Davis is more concerned with the messages in his art than with preparing works for exhibition.

About the Media
Davis works with a wide range of media. He is a ceramicist, photographer, jewelry maker, painter, and graphic artist. Drawing from an unlimited source of media allows Davis freedom of expression. He also relies a great deal on found objects to express the message of his artwork to the viewer.

About the Technique
Many of Davis's artistic works have come from an inquiry into his heritage. His art has been called "visual music." It is difficult to pinpoint one single technique for Davis. His methods are a reflection of the diversity he sees in the world. His ever-changing technique accommodates his ever-changing global perspective.

Artist Profile

Niki de Saint Phalle
1930–2002

Niki de Saint Phalle (niˊ kē da san fäl) was born Catherine Marie-Agnes in France, and moved to Connecticut with her family in 1933. They spent their summers in France, and her career was influenced by living in two cultures. As a child in New York, the artist often questioned authority and was transferred to different schools. After she graduated in 1948, de Saint Phalle moved to Paris and traveled throughout Europe where she was impressed with the idea that cathedrals were created by the collaboration of many artists. In 1960, she began her friendship and artistic partnership with Jean Tingueley, whom she married in 1971. Their artistic innovation and success brought them commissions from all over Europe and America. Eventually the artist settled in California.

About Art History

This artist became a member of the nouveau realists in 1961 and gained inspiration from its members. During the mid-1960s, she was commissioned for a number of public and private architectural projects. In 1978, she began the foundation for *Tarot Garden,* which she worked on for 20 years.

About the Artwork

Many of de Saint Phalle's oversized figures and sculptures were painted with bold colors and referenced the position of women in society, as evidenced in her *Nana* sculptures and *Sun God,* a vibrantly colored bird atop a 15-foot concrete arch. Her most famous work is her *Tarot Garden* in Tuscany; a collection of brightly painted public sculptures of the characters on tarot cards. One of these functional structures became her home for seven years while she worked on the garden.

About the Media

De Saint Phalle's large figural sculptures were generally made out of papier-mâché and painted in bright acrylic colors. Some of her *Nanas* were also made with yarn and cloth. Her functional sculptures for playgrounds and public display required concrete and architectural supplies for reinforcement. In her *Skinnys* she made totem pole-like sculptures suspended with colored lights and string.

About the Technique

Papier-mâché consists of paper pulp dipped in paste and then molded to a frame to harden. Usually the frames for larger sculptures were made of chicken wire. In her Target assemblages she threw darts of paint at her sculptures. Her most elaborate Target piece, or *Tir,* was a life-size plaster bull with paint and fireworks honoring the artist Salvador Dalí.

▲ **Edgar Degas.** (French). *Self Portrait.*
Sterling and Francine Clark Art Institute, Williamstown, Massachusetts.

Artist Profile

Edgar Degas
1834–1917

Edgar Degas (ed´ gär dā gä´) was born in Paris, France, to a wealthy family. He studied law for a short time before discovering his interest in painting. Degas studied briefly at the École des Beaux-Arts in Paris around 1855. He worked at an artist's studio and traveled widely to study art. His early work showed a concern with classical painting, in subject matter as well as composition. His themes always dealt with people and city life, especially dancers at the theater. After 1909, Degas turned to sculpture due to failing eyesight. He left many wax models of dancers and horses that were cast in bronze after his death.

About Art History

Degas joined the impressionist group and exhibited with them, even though he detested the name and never painted in a purely impressionistic style. He admired Italian Renaissance painters, such as Leonardo da Vinci. He also admired the French neoclassical painter Ingres, whose figures had the grace of Greek statues. In his own work Degas combined impressionism with the painting style of the Renaissance.

About the Artwork

Degas is famous for his portraits, especially those of ballet dancers. Unlike other impressionists, he enjoyed painting genre scenes of modern life. His painting of customers in a hat shop, for example, was unusual. At that time artists did not usually paint such ordinary places.

About the Media

Degas created oil paintings, pastel drawings, ink drawings, and bronze sculptures. He also produced a great number of lithographs, engravings, and monotypes.

About the Technique

Many impressionists painted outdoors and quickly. Degas chose to work slowly in his studio. He planned his pictures and completed sketches before he painted. He sometimes took paintings back after they had been sold so he could improve them. He applied paint sketchily to make his work look unplanned.

Degas wanted his subjects to look as if they did not know they were being painted. He cut figures off at the edges of the canvas to make his composition seem spontaneous and not posed. He also wanted viewers to feel as if they were part of the picture. For this reason, Degas included large, open spaces to welcome viewers into his paintings.

Artist Profile

Dorothy Djukulul
b. 1942

Dorothy Djukulul was born near Mulgurrum, Australia, and is a member of the aboriginal Ganalbingu clan. When she was young she attended a Methodist mission school, where the superintendent recognized her artistic talent and encouraged her to paint in the Western style. But every day after school her father and uncle would teach her the traditional way of painting on bark. After completing school Djukulul worked on the land and helped build stockyards until she moved far from her family. She worked as a baker and then returned to her home where she met and married Djardi Ashley, a well-known bark painter who supported Djukulul's desire to paint. She has become a prominent aboriginal artist and has participated in numerous exhibitions.

About Art History

Aboriginal art records the history and religion of the tribe, but only men are allowed to use the sacred symbols and designs in their work. When Djukulul's father and uncle taught her how to paint on bark, they did not pass along the knowledge of their sacred designs. However, her father, Nhulmarmar, changed his mind about this rule and passed along these traditional symbols to Djukulul in order to keep Ganalbingu art and stories alive. He consulted the tribal elders and received their permission for her to be allowed to paint the sacred designs. She now holds a special place in the aboriginal art world because she can paint symbols usually taboo to women.

About the Artwork

Djukulul is well-known for her *Flying Fox* paintings such as *Warrnyu*. The flat, patterned appearance of her work is typical of aboriginal art and is often created by an intricate series of dots placed meticulously on bark. Her *Flying Fox* designs incorporate images of blossoms, which represent the sweet-smelling fruit of the fox's diet.

About the Media

Djukulul uses traditional bush brushes and natural ochre pigments in her paintings. Bark is often her canvas, and she is highly respected for her original style.

About the Technique

The aboriginal canvas and bark paintings of today were originally painted in the sand and lasted only until the wind blew them away. Dorothy and her contemporaries use their artwork as a permanent record of heritage and tradition, sharing their history, stories, and religion through symbols and designs.

UNIT 5 • Lesson 2

Artist Profile

Richard Estes
b. 1936

Richard Estes (ri´ chərd es´ təs) was born in 1936 in Kewanee, Illinois. He attended the School of the Art Institute of Chicago, where he studied the works of artists such as Edgar Degas, Edward Hopper, and Thomas Eakins. Estes moved to New York City after graduating from college. He worked as a freelance illustrator, painting at night until he could begin his career as a full-time artist. His first solo show was held in 1968 at the Allan Stone Gallery in New York City. Estes was part of the photo-realism movement of the 1960s, which included Chuck Close and Duane Hanson.

About Art History

Photo-realism evolved from two longstanding art traditions: *trompe l'oeil* ("to fool the eye") painting and the meticulous detail of seventeenth-century Dutch painting. Photo-realism was characterized by an emphasis on sharp details, high finishes, and intensified realism, which caused viewers to question whether a painting was actually a photograph. Many photo-realistic paintings involved reflective surfaces, such as chrome, windows, or water. These surfaces added illusions of depth and realism to the compositions. Estes was influenced by the artists Canaletto, Charles Sheeler, and the Dutch painter Vermeer.

About the Artwork

In the 1960s, Estes became well known for his paintings of city streets and windows, often with one side of the street reflected in windows. One such painting is his 1968 *Telephone Booths*, which combines the reflective surfaces of steel doors and glass windows in an elaborate, geometric composition. His work is crisp and photographic, but often includes unrealistic perspectives.

About the Media

Estes works with oils on large canvases.

About the Technique

Estes works from photographs to complete his paintings. He declared that it was impossible to work from real life because too many elements would alter the composition and keep him from capturing accurate details. Weather, sunlight, traffic, and people in motion made it difficult for him to depict a single moment in time unless he used a camera. Sometimes he incorporates numerous pictures into one painting. With this technique, it has been said that he paints works that are more realistic than photographs.

Artist Profile

Philip Evergood
1901–1973

Philip Evergood (fi′ləp e′vər good) was born in New York City. His parents sent him to boarding schools in England and then to Cambridge University. He studied art briefly in Paris, France, but he taught himself to be a painter against his parents' wishes. For several years, Evergood traveled back and forth between Europe and the United States. He spent the 1930s, the years of the Great Depression, in America and used his paintings to protest against people's suffering. Evergood cared about human suffering and injustice, but he also had a temper and could be demanding and disagreeable. He married a ballet dancer, who lived with him only on weekends. He had no children, but loved his dogs. Evergood believed that his work would not be appreciated until after his death. He kept careful records of his life and art for those who might want to know about him. He died in a 1973 fire.

About Art History

Evergood's 1930s paintings were brutally realistic. They became less harsh later in his life. Many art critics did not compliment him, but he had great artistic talent. Evergood used his paintings to try to create a better society.

About the Media

Evergood began his career by painting murals for the Federal Art Project during the Great Depression. He worked mainly in oils.

About the Technique

Evergood painted in a fresh, simple style—almost like a child's. His work was sometimes thought of as raw and unfinished. He did not try to show depth—all his objects appear to be beside each other. In his early paintings he often used colors that clashed. Later he used more pleasing combinations.

Artist Profile

Janet Fish
b. 1938

Janet Fish (jan′ ət fish) earned two degrees in fine arts from Yale University but struggled to find work. For a while, she supported herself by painting bars of soap for a department store. Since then her large, lively still lifes have become much admired. Fish has taught at art schools across the nation. She now spends half her time in New York and half in Vermont.

About Art History

During the 1960s, Fish was part of a group of nontraditional painters. She is known as a realistic painter, but much of her work incorporates abstract qualities. For example, she might exaggerate the shapes of bottles and repeat those shapes within a painting.

About the Artwork

Fish's still lifes, landscapes, and portraits make ordinary objects seem extraordinary. She might begin painting a bottle of window cleaner or gummy candy, which she uses to create a fascinating combination of colors, contrasting surfaces, and light. She is especially interested in the effects of light, such as how it shines through a crystal bowl or on cut flowers.

About the Media

Fish's work includes both oil and watercolor paintings.

About the Technique

Fish carefully chooses and arranges the objects in her still lifes. She tries to feel a connection to the objects and to understand how the objects relate to one another. She is concerned about color, texture, and balance in her paintings. To increase the impact of her work she often paints objects three or four times larger than they really are. They usually fill the picture, crowding right up to the edge. Fish aims to paint still lifes that do not hold still.

Audrey Flack. (American). *Self-Portrait (The Memory).* 1958.
Oil on canvas. 50 × 34 inches (127 × 86.36 cm.).
Art Museum Miami University, Oxford, Ohio.

Artist Profile

Audrey Flack
b. 1931

Audrey Flack (ô´ drē flak) grew up in New York City and lives there still. She earned a fine arts degree from Yale. She also studied anatomy, the structure of the human body. This helps her make her paintings more realistic. Flack is married to a musician. Early in her career she painted while raising two daughters. She has also taught at Pratt Institute and New York University.

About Art History

Flack was a leader of the photorealists in the 1970s. She was one of the first artists to base paintings on photographs. However, she has also created abstract art. In fact, she does not follow any one art style. Instead, she paints and sculpts from her heart. She likes to reinvent her subjects in new ways.

About the Artwork

Flack has painted large abstract images, smaller realistic still lifes, portraits, landscapes, and seascapes. She has also created photorealistic paintings based on news stories. An example is *Kennedy Motorcade,* which focuses on the day President Kennedy was killed. Flack sometimes includes images of herself in her art. For instance, she placed a photo of herself in a painting of Marilyn Monroe. Her work often focuses on issues that are important to her, such as the role of women in society. Since 1983, Flack has focused on her sculpting because she likes its solid feel. Many of her sculptures look like ancient Greek goddesses in modern settings.

About the Media

Flack works in oils, acrylics, watercolors, and bronze sculpture.

About the Technique

In her photorealistic work Flack painted from slides projected onto canvas. At one time she used commercial slides and postcards. Later she worked from color slides she took herself. She uses an airbrush to apply paint.

UNIT 4 • Overview

Artist Profile

Aurelio and Francisco Flores

Aurelio Flores (ô rēl´ yō flôr´ ās) and his son Francisco (frən sēs´ cō) are sculpture artists living in Izucar de Matamoros in Puebla, Mexico. Their specialization is making large, complex ceramic candelabras for display in museums and restaurants. As a young man Aurelio Flores learned how to make heavy, ornate candelabras from his father. He worked in his father's workshop and studied his father's technique for creating a slightly smaller type of candelabra made specifically for decorating an altar at a service announcing the engagement of a young couple. Over time Aurelio Flores began making more complex, multitiered candleholders and taught the craft to his son Francisco. The Floreses occasionally make candelabras for display in private homes.

▲ **Aurelio and Francisco Flores.** (Mexico). *Candelabra.* c. 1980.

Hand molded, fired, painted; clay, paint, wire. $42 \times 26 \times 8\frac{1}{4}$ inches. ($106.68 \times 66.04 \times 20.96$ cm.).
Museum of International Folk Art, Santa Fe, New Mexico.

About Art History

Elaborately styled candleholders such as this candelabra were traditionally made to decorate church altars during wedding ceremonies in Mexico. After the wedding was over, the candelabra was given to the newlywed couple as a gift. Some candelabra were also carried in processions or used to decorate special altars during funeral services.

About the Artwork

This candelabra is very large, approximately 42 inches in height and 26 inches wide. It has seven layers, or tiers, each adorned with small ceramic figures of angels, saints, flowers, birds, and fruits. The entire piece has been painted in bright, festive colors and glazed with a shiny coating. A heavy ceramic base keeps the piece from tipping. Small projections at the top of the candelabra are the actual candleholders.

About the Media

This candelabra is made from hand-molded ceramic sculpted over a wire frame. Once dry, the piece was fired in a kiln and painted. The final process was to coat the finished piece in a glossy, protective glaze.

About the Technique

When designing and sculpting their huge candelabras, the Floreses use traditional religious icons, figures, and symbols. The candelabras made by the Floreses are complex and colorful. The candle-holding function has been reduced to a few small holders at the top of the piece. These candelabras are made to be much more decorative than functional.

Artist Profile

Thomas Gainsborough
1727–1788

British artist Thomas Gainsborough was born in Sudbury, Suffolk, in 1727. When he was about thirteen years old, Gainsborough went to London to study art. After finishing his education, he worked as a portrait artist in the town of Ipswich and later in Bath. In 1768, Gainsborough was elected a foundation member of the Royal Academy. He relocated permanently to London in 1774, where he focused on cultivating his luminous personal painting style. So exquisite and captivating were his portraits that he quickly became a sought after and respected artist throughout London's high society set, and he was a favorite painter of England's Royal Family.

About Art History

Gainsborough was an admirer of the famous seventeenth century Flemish painter Anthony van Dyck. Van Dyck often painted his subjects wearing clothing similar to the opulent blue suit worn by the young Jonathan Buttall in *Jonathan Buttall: The Blue Boy*. In the year 1921, the piece was sold to a wealthy art dealer for the highest sum ever paid for a single painting to that date.

About the Artwork

The painting *Jonathan Buttall: The Blue Boy* is quite large, measuring $70\frac{3}{4}$ inches in height and $48\frac{3}{4}$ inches in width. The painting depicts a young Jonathan Buttall, who was the son of a close friend of Thomas Gainsborough. The painting shows the boy wearing an elaborate blue suit, white stockings, and dress shoes adorned with thick ribbons. The suit is believed to have been a costume, not the everyday clothing of the boy, as the style of the suit dates it to well over one hundred years before the portrait was painted.

About the Media

Jonathan Buttall: The Blue Boy was painted in oil paints on canvas.

About the Technique

Jonathan Buttall: The Blue Boy was painted during a time when Thomas Gainsborough took up temporary residence in Bath, England, before settling in London in the year 1774. Because the subject of this work, Jonathan Buttall, was the son of the artist's close friend, it may be assumed that the boy was either asked to model for the painting or was hired to do so.

UNIT 1 • Lesson 6

Artist Profile

Al Held
b. 1928

Al Held (al held) was born in Brooklyn, New York, and grew up in the Bronx during the Great Depression. His family experienced difficult financial times, but Held found a way to attend the Art Students League from 1948 to 1949 and later the Academie de la Grande Chaumiere in Paris. He settled in New York and became known for his experiments in geometric form and line. From 1962 to 1978, Held was a member of the art faculty of Yale University and later moved to a studio near Woodstock, New York, where he lives today.

About Art History

Until 1959, Held painted in an abstract expressionistic style and was involved with the New York abstract expressionist movement. Between 1960 and 1967, his work began to shift away from abstract expressionism toward more tightly controlled geometric pieces, at times exploring the realms of analytic cubism through his clean, clear lines and reductive forms.

About the Artwork

Held's earlier work focused on the brushstroke, laden heavily with paint and emotion. As he experimented with this style, he found the need to reduce its busy visual appearance. He began to structure his brushwork by constructing bands of color in impasto, painting wet into wet and simplifying his color palette. His geometric forms were often black and white and used perspective as a means of form. By employing depth of field and layering as actual forms, Held brought the painting's plane closer to the viewer. He wanted to develop a means of expressing a multiplicity and complexity in his paintings and chose to use random multiple perspectives that overlapped each other. Often he leaves the edges of his pieces unpainted so the geometric forms and layers of perspective seem to float on the canvas and jump out at the viewer.

About the Media

Held's large, oversized paintings are created in both oils and acrylics on canvas. Held was commissioned to paint murals, one of which can be found in the Empire State Plaza in Albany, New York. This mural is a good example of his simplified geometric forms and earlier black and white palette.

About the Technique

Held's paintings are about layering—both of his images and his paint. As he paints, layers of forms appear. If he is not happy with the layering, he sands the paint down and begins painting new lines and shapes. This sanding keeps the surface of the canvas very smooth, so his finished paintings appear to be one large composition instead of many combined revisions.

Artist Profile

John Hoover
b. 1919

John Hoover (jän hōō′ vər) was born in Cordova, Alaska, to an Aleut-Russian mother and a German father. Growing up, he spent a lot of time fishing and making art, and his early involvement in boat building inspired his interest in sculpture. Hoover has always been fascinated with traditional Northwest Coast Native American carvings, and continues to reference them in his work today. As one of the most respected contemporary Native American sculptors, Hoover has exhibited around the country and continues to make art at his home in Washington.

About Art History

In the 1950s, Hoover began his artistic career as a painter, although he was also a fisherman, taxi driver, drummer, and sailor. His artwork turned toward sculpture in the 1960s when he began working collaboratively on a 58-foot Alaskan fishing boat. His earlier woodwork was traditional and used primarily rectangular boards. These later evolved into carved panels that, when hinged together, created a unified composition. Hoover continues to be inspired by the bright colors and storytelling characteristics of Northwest Coast Native American carvings that represent ancient myths and Native cultures. His travels to the Philippines, Taiwan, and Japan introduced him to the woodworking techniques of those cultures and had a surrealistic influence on his carving.

About the Artwork

A predominant theme in Hoover's work is the transformation of animals to humans and humans to animals. *Shamanism,* a cultural practice involving communication with spirits, is also factored into his work. Hoover bases much of his art on myths or legends and also creates his own artistic narratives, often including the representation of a human form in his carvings. Graceful forms of birds and sea life appear in his depictions of the Aleut and Aluttiq cultures.

About the Media

Hoover carves his sculptures and panels from red cedar wood, which is also known as the "tree of life" to Northwest Coast Native Americans. In addition to cedar work, he has created some bronze sculptures. One of his recent commissions involved an installation for the Alaska Native Medical Center in Anchorage, for which he sculpted 34 snow geese to surround the building's rotunda.

About the Technique

Hoover's triptychs, or hinged wooden panels, are carved on both sides so they will reveal one image when opened and a second image when closed. He creates his sculptures through a process of reduction, carving slowly from a block of wood until he reaches a desired shape.

Edward Hopper. (American). *Self-Portrait.* 1903.
Charcoal on paper. 18½ × 12 inches (47 × 30.5 cm.).
National Portrait Gallery, Smithsonian Institution, Washington, D.C.

Artist Profile

Edward Hopper
1882–1967

Edward Hopper (ed´ wərd hä´ pər) was born in Nyack, New York. He attended the New York School of Art and made three trips to Europe to study art. He worked as an illustrator in New York City and eventually opened a studio in Greenwich Village. Hopper married another painter, Josephine Nivison, who helped arrange his first exhibition. They spent their summers on an island off the Maine coast, on Cape Cod, and at other East Coast locations. These spots became the settings of many of Hopper's paintings.

About Art History

Hopper was one of the finest realistic painters of his time. Although his style was realistic, he often adjusted reality to suit the image he had in mind. For example, he changed the size or shape of objects to create a better balance, or left out the trees or a street near a house he was painting.

About the Artwork

Hopper's works emphasize the loneliness of modern life. Although he lived in a crowded city, his scenes were usually empty of people. He preferred subjects that included water, such as lighthouses, rivers, and bridges. Another favorite subject was a large, old house, often surrounded by dead trees. Hopper occasionally added one or more people to such scenes.

About the Media

Hopper painted primarily with oils. He also made many watercolor paintings. His drawings were all studies that he used for his paintings. Hopper used charcoal, pencil, pen and ink, and conté crayon to create his drawings.

About the Technique

Early in his career Hopper often worked in the back seat of his car, which served as his studio on wheels. He began by outlining a scene with a pale pencil. Then he painted without planning, focusing on the structure and the light in the scene. In one painting, for example, he used a delicate, musty light to indicate early morning on a beach. In his famous painting *Nighthawks* a bright light that creates hard-edged shadows reveals a group of sad people at a lunch counter late at night. Hopper usually painted his watercolors outdoors.

Artist Profile

Joseph Jean-Gilles
b. 1943

Born in Haiti, Joseph Jean-Gilles (zhō´ zəf zhän gil lē´) now lives in Florida, but his native land is never far from his mind. He studied art at Centre d'Art in Port-au-Prince, Haiti, until 1967, and has been painting scenes of his homeland ever since. Jean-Gilles has had a number of exhibitions in New York and Washington, D.C., as well as in Haiti. His paintings hang in museums including New York's Museum of Modern Art and the Art Museum of the Americanas in Port-au-Prince.

About Art History

Jean-Gilles is considered a primitive painter, much like the nineteenth-century French painter Rousseau. Jean-Gilles has gained skills that take him beyond a spontaneous recording of what he sees or imagines to a carefully planned and sophisticated portrayal of his ideas.

About the Artwork

Haitian Landscape is an excellent example of Jean-Gilles's art. He paints the tropical landscape of his homeland in an idealized way. For example, his trees differ only slightly in shape, and his human figures are like dolls but are almost faceless. This stylized approach makes the painting seem like a fairy tale, which expresses Jean-Gilles's feelings about Haiti. His carefully tended fields show the human influence on the landscape and stress the interdependence of people and nature. With everything in its proper place and nothing amiss, Jean-Gilles reminds viewers that everyone is looking for a place in the universe. His ideal view of Haiti suggests hope for the future of this politically torn island.

About the Media

Jean-Gilles works mainly in oils on canvas.

About the Technique

In his paintings, Jean-Gilles overlaps objects to show the great variety in the lush landscape. He has studied the trees and plants of Haiti and arranges them into precise patterns. Jean-Gilles combines vivid colors with interrelated forms.

Artist Profile

Isabel John

Isabel John (i´ zə bel jän) is the best-known weaver of Navajo pictorial rugs today. John probably learned how to weave from an aunt or grandmother because this skill is traditionally passed down from mother to daughter. She has been weaving for many years and is now teaching this skill to others. She lives on the Navajo reservation in the northeastern Arizona city of Many Farms.

About Art History

Weaving is an important part of Navajo culture and history. Isabel John is well known for her pictorial weavings. Pictorial weavings, also known as *tapestries,* are a recent development in Navajo weaving. Earlier Navajo weavings showed only geometric designs and simple patterns. The earliest example of a Navajo pictorial design was a blanket belonging to a Cheyenne warrior in 1864. This blanket's design was almost completely geometric but included a bird in each corner. Today's pictorial weavings show images of horses, flags, houses, landscapes, and many other objects. Some tell stories about Navajo life.

About the Artwork

John creates weavings showing scenes from everyday life on the Navajo reservation. She creates visual recordings of the history and traditions of the Navajo. Some popular imagery in her artwork includes logos, animals, buildings, automobiles, trucks, wagons, road signs, and trains. Her weavings are extremely detailed and technically complex.

About the Media

John uses wool from sheep, commercial and natural dyes, and a handmade wooden loom to make her weavings.

About the Technique

John shears wool from sheep for her weavings. Then she cards, washes, spins, and dyes the wool. She makes her weavings completely by hand on an upright loom. John starts a weaving with only an idea of how she wants the finished tapestry to look. She does not draw her design on paper before she weaves it. A tapestry can take up to a year to weave.

Artist Profile

Calvin Jones
b. 1934

Born in Illinois, Calvin Jones (kal´ vin jōnz) began exhibiting his work while he was still in elementary school in Chicago. After graduation from high school, he received a full scholarship to the Art Institute of Chicago, where he studied drawing, painting, and illustration. Jones worked for 17 years as an illustrator and graphic designer. He won many awards for his work before deciding to paint full-time. Since then, he has gained widespread recognition for his ability to share the African American experience through modern art.

About Art History

In his art, Jones combines abstraction with reality. Some of his work involves hard edge, color field, and minimal art. These traditional styles from Africa, Asia, and the Americas were not incorporated into Western art until the twentieth century, and they became popular during the 1950s and 1960s. These styles use geometric shapes and colors to express ideas.

About the Artwork

Jones focuses on abstract images of the African American experience, but his work also stresses that we are all one people. He creates easel paintings and murals that reflect his cultural heritage. Sometimes Jones includes patterns that remind viewers of African textiles, as he did in his painting *Maskamorphosis I*. In this painting he used symbolic shapes to form masks. His images seem both abstract and realistic.

About the Media

Jones works in mixed media, including oils and acrylics.

About the Technique

Jones combines bright colors and textures with bold designs of intersecting lines and geometric shapes.

Artist Profile

Fred Kabotie
1900–1986

Fred Kabotie (fred kä bō´ tē) was born in Arizona to a traditional Hopi family. He first started drawing on rocks in his father's fields. Later the government forced him, like other Native American children, to attend the Santa Fe Indian School. The school's superintendent recognized Kabotie's artistic skills and encouraged him to become an artist. In 1920, Kabotie became the first Hopi to be recognized nationally for his art. In 1937, he returned to his hometown and began to teach his version of Hopi art at the new high school. His teaching and work influenced generations of Hopi artists. Even the French government recognized Kabotie for his contributions to Native American art. His son Michael has also become an artist who promotes traditional Hopi arts and culture.

About Art History

Traditionally, most Hopi painting was done on walls during ceremonies. At the Santa Fe Indian School, Kabotie was encouraged to break with this tradition and paint pictures of the ceremonies themselves. Kabotie learned to paint in a realistic style using European techniques. He used shading to give depth to objects, pay close attention to detail, and emphasize color. Over the years Kabotie began to include ancient Hopi images in his paintings, which are more stylized than most of his other work.

About the Artwork

Kabotie often painted the rituals and ceremonies of his people as in the watercolor *Social Dance*. Sometimes he returned to the two-dimensional painting style of his ancestors, as in *The Legend of the Snake Clan*. This work is painted on animal hide and includes symbols for people and nature.

About the Media

Kabotie worked in both oils and watercolors.

About the Technique

Kabotie approached each painting as a problem to be solved, not a task to be repeated. His painting style and techniques changed over the years. He went from using detailed brushstrokes to painting more abstract images.

Artist Profile

Wassily Kandinsky
1866–1944

Wassily Kandinsky (va sēl´ ē kan din´ skē) first tried painting as a teenager in his native Russia. Even then he felt that each color had a mysterious life of its own. He was still drawn to colors and painting while he studied law and economics in college, but he believed that art was "a luxury forbidden to a Russian." In time, he moved to Germany, studied art, and began his career. Throughout his life Kandinsky moved back and forth between Russia and Germany. In 1933 he settled in France after Nazi storm troopers labeled his painting style "degenerate."

About Art History

Kandinsky was a pioneer in the pure abstract painting style—a combination of color and form with no subject matter. He did not give a title to a painting he did in 1910, but others called it the *First Abstract Watercolour.* Kandinsky felt that trying to paint recognizable objects distracted artists from their real jobs of expressing ideas and emotions. He believed communicating through painting was similar to communicating with music. He often gave his paintings titles that were musical and abstract, such as *Improvisation 30.*

About the Artwork

It is possible to identify landscapes and objects in some of Kandinsky's early paintings, but his later work was entirely abstract. Only occasionally during World War I did Kandinsky include cannons and other recognizable objects in his work.

About the Media

Kandinsky worked in oils, watercolors, and India ink.

About the Technique

Kandinsky did not try to show the essence of his subjects because he had none. Instead, he attempted to make forms and colors take on meaning separate from the physical world. His work often impresses even viewers who are not certain what the paintings mean.

UNIT 1 • Lesson 2

Artist Profile

Paul Klee
1879–1940

Paul Klee (paul klā) was born into a musical Swiss family. His family hoped he also would become a musician. At age five his grandmother gave him his first box of pencils. He thought of himself as an artist from then on, but he continued to have an interest in music. Klee played his violin for an hour nearly every morning of his life. He married a pianist. As an adult Klee still drew in a childlike way. Klee believed that childlike drawings were the most creative and original. He was not trying to share his ideas through his work. He just wanted to explore his imagination. Klee could use either hand proficiently when painting.

About Art History

At first, art critics ignored Klee's work. Then they realized that his small, charming, playful pictures were filled with ideas and meaning. Different people find different meanings in Klee's pictures. For many people this adds to the value of his work.

About the Artwork

Klee studied nature and often began his paintings with an image from nature. Then he would let his imagination take over.

About the Media

Klee painted with watercolors and other materials on paper, canvas, silk, linen, and burlap. He liked to experiment; for example, he did one picture with black paste on burlap.

About the Technique

Color was important to Klee. He once said, "Color and I are one; I am a painter." In his watercolors Klee used thin layers of pale color. This technique made his pictures gently shimmer like pavement under a hot sun. Klee used color the way a musician uses sound. He tried to touch the feelings of his viewers. Klee said that he learned more about painting from the musicians Bach and Mozart than he did from other visual artists.

Artist Profile

Lundin Kudo

Lundin Kudo (lun´ dēn koo´ dō) creates pear sculptures so realistic that a viewer might not realize they are made of clay and take a bite. Kudo uses the pear shape in much of her work, and she explores the different textures, shapes, and colors of everyday objects through her art. She also uses color and texture to explore subjects, such as her life-size sculptures of middle-aged women.

About Art History

Kudo first studied art in a private studio in Seville, Spain, from 1959 to 1960. Nine years later she earned her degree from the University of Michigan and then moved to Florida, where she continues to live and work today. She has created her own business from her clay work, and works on commission. People buying her artwork can sometimes choose how they would like their sculptures to appear. Several of Kudo's works are even covered in gold.

About the Artwork

Japanese koi, the world's most popular ornamental pond fish, are often called *living jewels* or *swimming flowers*. Kudo depicts the fish in a realistic way and sculpts them to appear as though they are swimming in water, with the sunlight shimmering on their iridescent scales. Her clay piece *Gin Matsuba* represents a kind of Japanese koi and is painted in the same warm glowing colors found in real fish.

About the Media

Kudo makes batik cloths, jewelry, and paintings, but she is best known for her clay fruit, figures, and fish. Her affinity for pears is evident in her life-size human figures that feature pear-shaped bodies. Pears, peppers, honeybell oranges, apples, mangoes, and other fruits and vegetables are represented in Kudo's work, which can be found in public and private collections around the world.

About the Technique

Partially eaten pears and peppers are often found in Kudo's studio, because they are the models for her realistic clay sculptures. She builds her work by hand and also uses slip-casting, which allows her to make multiple versions of the same form, though each finished piece is unique. The sculptures are bisque and glaze fired, which means they are fired before and after glaze is applied. Then they are fired again to create iridescent and gold coloration and a unique final appearance.

Artist Profile

Jacob Lawrence
1917–2000

Jacob Lawrence (jā´ kəb lär´ ənz) had parents who met on their migration to the North. His father was born in South Carolina, and his mother in Virginia. Lawrence was born in Atlantic City, New Jersey, in 1917. The family finally settled in Harlem in 1929 at the end of the Harlem Renaissance. Because his mother worked all day, she enrolled Lawrence in the Harlem Art Workshop after school to keep him out of trouble. He had many excellent teachers there, including Charles Alston. Lawrence won a scholarship to the American Artists School. He taught at New York's Pratt Institute from 1958 to 1965. From 1970, he taught at the University of Washington in Seattle, where he also served as head of the art department. He won many awards in his lifetime, including the Presidential Medal of Arts.

About Art History

Lawrence's paintings not only contribute to the art world, they also add to our knowledge of African American history. Lawrence painted African American heroes, such as Harriet Tubman and Frederick Douglass.

About the Artwork

Lawrence's most famous work is a series of 60 paintings called *Migration of the Negro*. The paintings tell a story which begins at a train station in the South and ends at a station in the North. The scenes he chose to paint focus on the struggle of leaving one life for another and the search for freedom and dignity. His paintings did not overlook the harshness and violence that was part of this migration. During World War II he served in the U.S. Coast Guard and created a series of paintings about his experiences. They were exhibited by the Museum of Modern Art in 1944.

About the Media

Lawrence painted on paper with *gouache,* an opaque watercolor paint, similar to tempera paint used in schools. It covers the paper with a smooth, matte coat. He was also a printmaker.

About the Technique

Lawrence said a lot about his subjects with only a few lines and carefully chosen colors. He used many neutral colors, such as taupe, mocha, and charcoal, and balanced them with splashes of bright color.

Artist Profile

Fernand Léger
1881–1955

Fernand Léger (fer nän´ lā zhā´) was the son of French peasants, but his art strayed far from the rural countryside. He spent his life exploring the modern industrial world from an artist's point of view. Perhaps his early training in an architect's office encouraged his fascination with what came to be known as "machine art." Léger combined the cubist painting style with images from the industrial world. The people in his pictures, broken into flat planes, seem more like robots than humans.

About Art History

Léger was strongly influenced by Cézanne and became a cubist painter. Like other cubists, Léger looked at his subjects from several angles and combined the angles in the same picture. For example, he might show the top, bottom, and sides of a subject in one painting. To do this, cubists broke a subject into surfaces, or planes. To some people, cubist paintings seem to be cubes or boxes falling through space. Léger often showed buildings as cones and cylinders that looked like machine parts. Toward the end of Léger's life, his art became increasingly abstract and geometric.

About the Artwork

One of Léger's favorite subjects was the city. He was fascinated by the combined effects of large billboards, flashing lights, noisy traffic, and the movement of people. Léger also painted people in motion in two series called *The Divers* and *The Cyclists*. In addition, he used the cubist style to paint circus scenes and family picnics.

About the Media

Besides creating oil paintings, Léger worked in ceramics and stained glass. He also designed sets for ballets and motion pictures, and was the director of the short film *Ballet Mécanique*.

About the Technique

In his early paintings, Léger used bright colors and heavy black outlines. Later he painted abstract color patterns and drew outlined subjects over them.

Artist Profile

Arthur Lismer
1885–1969

Although Arthur Lismer (är´ thər lis´ mər) was born in England he is generally considered a Canadian artist. He studied art in England and Belgium and then moved to Canada in 1911 to take a job as a commercial artist. Outgoing and outspoken, Lismer helped form the Group of Seven. This group of young artists painted the Canadian landscape they loved so much. They also encouraged each other to experiment with painting styles and held exhibitions together. Lismer taught art and served as the principal of art schools in Quebec and Nova Scotia. In addition, he set up children's art centers at the Art Gallery of Toronto and the Montreal Museum of Fine Arts.

About Art History

As a member of the Group of Seven, Lismer led the way in developing an imaginative approach to painting that matched the wild Canadian countryside. He also had a long-lasting influence on art education for children. He did not think all young people should become artists, but he did want them all to have the opportunity to use their imaginations and express themselves through art.

About the Artwork

In his own art Lismer focused on Georgian Bay in Ontario. On his first boat trip there he and his wife and child became stranded on an island in the bay during a storm. After that he painted the area many times. For example, *A September Gale, Georgian Bay* is a close-up of a tree being thrashed by a storm. During World War I Lismer painted war-related images such as camouflaged ships.

About the Media

Lismer painted primarily in oils and sketched in pencil and ink.

About the Technique

During his lifetime Lismer greatly improved his skills. His early paintings have been described as "crude" and "muddy in color." However, in his later work, he used bold, slashing brushstrokes and carefully chosen colors to show the forces of nature at work.

Artist Profile

Tom Loeser
b. 1956

Furniture artist Tom Loeser (tom lō´ sər) was born in 1956 in Boston, Massachusetts. He began exhibiting shortly after he graduated from college in 1982 and was immediately recognized by critics for a dynamic use of color in his three-dimensional sculptures. Among other shows, he was part of a group exhibition about resource conservation and the use of recycled materials and lesser-used wood species. This exhibit drew attention to the ways an artist can affect environmental change and maintain a healthy relationship with nature.

About Art History

Loeser's sculptures reference classical architecture and historic art like the geometric paintings of Piet Mondrian. Loeser creates *functional art,* which is always utilitarian. Functional art can be an article of furniture or an object. Loeser's art is included in museums in Massachusetts, New York, and North Carolina. He is currently a professor of art at the University of Wisconsin.

About the Artwork

Wall cabinets, chairs, benches, chests, tables, and abstract prints are some of Loeser's creations. He uses a variety of styles, sometimes emphasizing geometric shapes as in *Folding Chair,* and other times focusing on sweeping, organic forms as in *Scoring, Rocking, Rolling, Resting, Storing.* Surface color and texture are important to Loeser's work. Loeser uses muted, monochromatic pastels and strong, energetic hues in his work. He draws attention to color by creating different surface textures as in his mahogany sculpture *Four by Four.*

About the Media

Loeser uses various types of carved wood in his hand-painted functional sculptures. He also uses woodcut and silkscreen prints in his work. In his print *2D or not 2D,* the shapes can be cut out to form a free-standing paper chest.

About the Technique

Loeser makes many sketches and measurements of his functional furniture before preparing to carve or cut material. Some of his surfaces seem to be worn down, like driftwood. He creates this appearance by sanding the painted wood. He cuts precise, angular shapes with tools such as tablesaws, bandsaws, and jigsaws.

UNIT 5 • Lesson 2

Artist Profile

René Magritte
1898–1967

René Magritte (rə nē´ mə grēt´) was born in Belgium at the end of the nineteenth century. After studying art in Brussels, he worked briefly in a wallpaper factory. The influence of his time at this factory is sometimes evident in his patterned paintings. Magritte had a mischievous attitude, and displayed an avant-garde, poetic energy. He directed this energy into numerous creations and was honored with retrospective exhibitions in both Europe and the United States.

About Art History

Surrealists valued fantastic, absurd and poetic images. They also valued the artwork of children or the untrained amateur artist because they were thought to create from pure impulse and to be free from convention. Although Magritte did not paint in a childish hand, he was a contemporary of fellow surrealist artists Joan Miró, André Breton, Jean Arp, Salvador Dalí, and Paul Eluard. In both group and solo exhibits Magritte's work was shown in galleries in Brussels, Paris, New York, and London, and is represented in many museums.

About the Artwork

The poetic nature of language interested Magritte, and he admired the way it combined with a visual image to make viewers question the context and intent of his paintings. *La Vie des Aire (The Voice of Space)* seems to ask these questions. Its floating spheres and landscape contradict reason and tell a story that cannot be easily read. Magritte didn't abandon realism in his paintings but transferred realistic objects, such as a tree, chair, or clock, into a dreamlike environment or behavior. In *The Fall* he painted men wearing overcoats and bowler hats falling from the sky onto a town below. Pattern and a muted palette make their way into a number of Magritte's works as well as some of his commissioned murals in Brussels.

About the Media

Magritte worked with oil paints on canvas.

About the Technique

Magritte employed free association in the philosophical interpretation of his paintings. He would make sketches of his subjects and then use light brushstrokes on his canvases to create a dreamlike airiness.

Artist Profile

Sylvia Plimack Mangold
b. 1938

Sylvia Plimack Mangold (sil´ vē ə pli´ mak man´ gōld) was born in New York City. She attended several art schools and earned a degree in fine arts from Yale University. In 1974, she had her first show, and her work has been much admired ever since. Mangold taught at the School of Visual Arts in New York City. She is married to artist Robert Mangold, and they have two sons. She lives on a 150-acre farm in Washingtonville, New York.

About Art History
Mangold's work has been called realistic. However her work does not fit easily into a specific category because her realistic paintings still have an abstract quality.

About the Artwork
Mangold's artwork reflects her surroundings. Early in her career, she painted images of floors and rooms. Later she painted scenes outside the studio window on her farm. Since 1983, Mangold has painted landscapes around her home. She has made many paintings of trees, often making a single tree the focus of a painting.

About the Media
This artist works in oils on canvas and linen and in watercolors, acrylics, pencil, ink, and pastels. She also creates prints.

About the Technique
Mangold tries to make her paintings seem three-dimensional, like sculptures. She uses rulers and masking tape while creating her paintings. She often leaves the used tape on the canvas as part of the picture. Mangold usually sketches her subjects outdoors and completes the paintings in her studio.

Artist Profile

Henri Matisse
1869–1954

Henri Matisse (än´ rē ma tēs´) was the son of a middle-class couple in the north of France. He was not interested in art while he was in school. After high school his father sent him to law school in Paris. When he was 21 an appendicitis attack changed his life. Because he had to spend a long time in the hospital, his mother brought him a paint box to help him pass the time. Matisse eventually convinced his father to let him drop out of law school and study art. Matisse married and started a family soon after. His paintings were not selling, so he worked for a decorator and his wife opened a hat shop. During the last years of his life he suffered from arthritis. Unable to hold a brush in his hands, he devoted his efforts to making paper cutouts from papers painted to his specifications, and he created fantastic, brightly colored shapes. Unlike many other artists, he was internationally famous during his lifetime.

About Art History

In 1905, Matisse and his friends exhibited a painting style that showed strong emotionalism, wild colors, and distortion of shape. They were called *les fauves,* or "the wild beasts," and they experimented with intense, sometimes violent colors. Without letting their work become abstract, Matisse and other fauvist painters tested the bounds of reality.

About the Artwork

Matisse painted still lifes, room interiors, and landscapes. His paintings of dancers and human figures were generally more concerned with expressive shapes than an accurate representation of anatomy.

About the Media

Matisse painted primarily with oils, and also created many prints. Later in life he worked with cut paper.

About the Technique

Matisse worked with bold, intense colors. He simplified and distorted shapes for expressive qualities. He was most interested in the way visual elements were organized.

Artist Profile

Ayako Miyawaki
b. 1905

During World War II Japanese artist Ayako Miyawaki (ä ē kō mē yä wä kē) spent much of her time in bomb shelters. As soon as the war ended she began to experiment with fabric art. She never attended art school. She created her first fabric picture using appliqué in 1945 at age 40. In 1950, she had her first public exhibition—in a candy store. Since then her work has become popular. It is exhibited in Japan and the United States. Her husband was a teacher and painter, and Miyawaki has several children.

About Art History

Miyawaki's work followed a long tradition in Japanese art. It focused on showing appreciation for beauty. Appliqué is an ancient art created as early as 200 B.C. Miyawaki's technique of using string in her appliqué also dates back to ancient times.

About the Artwork

Miyawaki portrays natural objects such as fish, fruit, flowers, and vegetables in her designs. One of her appliqué works, *The Red Crab,* combines red and green fabrics with smooth and rough textures. The playful design seems ancient.

About the Media

Appliqué is also called *rag art.* Appliqué artists combine pieces of fabric to make pictures and designs. Miyawaki uses brightly colored fabrics with Japanese designs. Sometimes she dyes worn fabric into the vivid colors she likes.

About the Technique

Miyawaki works without using patterns. She cuts fabric pieces freehand and sews or glues them onto her canvases. She often combines different textures. She also uses the threads that attach the pieces of fabric as part of her design. In many of her works the fabric pieces look like splashes of paint on a canvas.

Artist Profile

Claude Monet
1840–1926

Claude Monet (klōd mō nā´) did not want to be a painter as a young man in France. He was already well paid for drawing caricatures of tourists. Painter Eugene Boudin saw talent in Monet's exaggerated drawings and encouraged him to paint. Although artists were "supposed" to paint in studios, Boudin urged Monet to paint outside in the open air. There Monet learned to capture his first impressions on canvas. He recorded these impressions during a long and productive life. His greatest wish was to "mingle more closely with nature."

About Art History

Monet made a large contribution to the development of impressionism through his ideas and paintings. Unlike most painters before him, Monet painted outdoors. He made careful observations of subject matter, studying the changes in appearance due to light and weather. In the first impressionist exhibition, Monet included a work titled *Impression: Sunrise*. A critic, ridiculing the colors, strange distortion of shapes, and loose brushstrokes, derived the name *impressionism* from this title. The term *impressionism* was soon accepted and used by the public to describe this new style of painting.

About the Artwork

Monet painted landscapes and people but especially loved scenes that included water. At one time he had a floating studio. He filled a rowboat with art supplies and painted in the shade of a striped awning. Toward the end of his life, Monet painted huge landscapes of the garden and lily ponds near his home in Giverny, France.

About the Media

Although he made sketches later in life, Monet created mostly oil paintings. By the 1870s, Monet eliminated black from his palette, replacing it with blue.

About the Technique

Monet often began a painting by covering the canvas with a background color. Then, he dabbed paint here and there until shapes became recognizable. He was fascinated by the way the same color could look different at certain times of the day or during particular weather conditions. He often painted the same subjects over and over again to capture this in his paintings. Examples of motifs he painted include Rouen Cathedral, poplars, haystacks, and water lilies.

Artist Profile

Philip Moulthrop
b. 1947

Philip Moulthrop (fil´ ip mōl´ thrəp) was born in 1947 in Atlanta, Georgia. His father, Edward Moulthrop, is also an artist, and the two are widely known for their elegant wooden bowls. Moulthrop regards his art as a means of revealing the beauty and texture of wood and wants his viewers to enjoy his work without having to be told what it means or how it was made. In addition to being a nationally acclaimed artist, Moulthrop is also a lawyer. He works from his studio in Marietta, Georgia, and has works displayed in such prestigious locations as the High Museum of Art in Atlanta, Georgia, and the Smithsonian Institution and the White House, both in Washington D.C.

About Art History

Woodturning has been a craft for hundreds of years, reaching back to ancient Egypt. Its utilitarian purposes did not move toward art until the last 60 years. New developments in tools, metal technology, wood preserving chemicals, and finishes have allowed wood turners to expand their styles and sizes of work. Larger pieces of wood can now be used to make a single-block creation.

About the Artwork

Moulthrop is famous for his open-shaped bowls and innovative departures from the traditional method of turning a piece from a single block of wood. This style results in lathe-turned bowls that are composed of hundreds of end grain sections instead of the continuous grain of one kind of wood. In *White Pine Mosaic Bowl* Moulthrop used cross sections of white pine preserved and suspended in resin to create the bowl's repeated pattern of circles. This piece is now in the White House. Smooth lines and perfected finishes characterize Moulthrop's work, as well as the unique wood grain and coloration of each piece. He does not carve the surfaces of his bowls, because he wants the wood's natural beauty to serve as their only embellishment.

About the Media

Moulthrop uses only domestic wood from southeastern forests. Sometimes the logs he uses weigh more than 1500 pounds. The woods range in color from regular browns and creams to yellows and reds. Moulthrop learned blacksmithing from his father, with whom he builds many of his own tools.

About the Technique

Moulthrop's technique is called *green turning*. He rough-shapes the bowl while the wood is still wet, and then soaks the piece for two to three months in polyethylene glycol, which prevents cracking. This technique protects the piece, but also changes the quality of the wood so that traditional finishes such as oil or wax cannot be used. Philip solved this problem by refining a high-gloss epoxy coating that his father developed.

Artist Profile

Louise Nevelson
1900–1988

Louise Nevelson (loo ĕz´ ne´ vəl sən), one of the most important and successful American sculptors of the twentieth century, was born in Kiev, Russia. Her family resettled in Rockland, Maine, when she was five years old. As a child she began assembling wood scraps from her father's contracting business. Her education was rich and varied, including music, theatre, dance, and visual art. She studied in New York, New York and Paris, France. At first she made both paintings and sculptures, but eventually concentrated on sculpture, which she exhibited irregularly from the 1930s onward. It was not until the late 1950s that she began to receive critical acclaim. Before her death, she had received more public commissions than any other living sculptor.

About Art History

During the twentieth century the art of Africa, Oceania, and pre-Columbian America was studied. Artists also began to take interest in the visual and mythic powers these cultural artifacts possessed. Louise Nevelson was influenced by tribal and Mayan art. Her work has a modern, totemic power that links contemporary art styles to ancient civilizations.

About the Artwork

By painting her sculptures all black, white, or gold, Nevelson transformed the typical meanings of her found elements. These elements are combined to express both formal and thematic concerns. Toward the end of her career she worked with more abstract, geometric shapes. Many of her large public sculptures are made from steel.

About the Media

Nevelson used found wooden objects to create many of her works.

About the Technique

The paint on Nevelson's sculptures unifies the many shapes, but allows the grain of the wood to show through, giving liveliness to the abstract forms.

Artist Profile

Georgia O'Keeffe
1887–1986

Georgia O'Keeffe (jôr´ jə ō kēf´) was born in Sun Prairie, Wisconsin. At the age of ten she began taking private art lessons, but the thing she liked most was experimenting with art at home. By 13, she had decided to become an artist. She trained under experts and won many prizes for her art. For years she challenged the art world with her unique vision. She eventually became famous for her spectacular, larger-than-life paintings of natural objects, including flowers, animal skulls, and shells. She loved nature, especially the desert of New Mexico, where she spent the last half of her life. O'Keeffe was married to the famous American photographer Alfred Stieglitz and appears in many of his photographs. In 1997, a Georgia O'Keeffe Museum opened in Santa Fe, New Mexico. It is the first museum in the United States devoted exclusively to the work of a major female artist.

About Art History

Stieglitz promoted modern artists and photographers from Europe and America through a magazine called *Camera Work* and a gallery known as "291." O'Keeffe and the circle of artists she met through Stieglitz were pioneers of modernism in the United States. She took subjects into her imagination and altered and simplified their appearances. She expressed her emotions through her vivid paintings.

About the Artwork

O'Keeffe's artwork features bold, colorful, abstract patterns and shapes. She most often painted natural forms such as flowers and bleached bones, pulling them out of their usual environments. She never painted portraits but sometimes painted landscapes.

About the Media

O'Keeffe used oils and watercolors for her paintings. She used pastels, charcoal, and pencil for her drawings.

About the Technique

O'Keeffe worked in dazzling, jewel-toned colors. She chose unusual perspectives, such as very close up or far away. She also enlarged the scale of her subjects.

Artist Profile

Pablo Picasso
1881–1973

Pablo Picasso (pä´ blō pi kä´ sō) was born in Málaga, Spain. He did poorly in school but his father, an art teacher, taught him to draw and paint. Picasso learned quickly. When he was only 14 he had a painting accepted for an exhibition. Picasso moved to Paris, France when he was 18. At the time he was very poor. Thieves stole what little he had, yet they left his now valuable drawings. In time the outgoing Picasso made many friends. Among them were the American writers Ernest Hemingway and Gertrude Stein and the Russian composer Igor Stravinsky. Picasso painted at night and slept late most mornings. He worked hard his entire life. He completed 200 paintings the year he turned 90.

About Art History

Picasso was one of the most influential artists of the 1900s. He experimented with many styles and created new ones. He invented the style known as cubism. He took 18 months to paint his first cubist picture, *Les Demoiselles d'Avignon,* which shows five women from several angles. Other artists were soon copying his style.

About the Artwork

Picasso's paintings changed as his life changed. When he was poor, he painted sad pictures in shades of blue. This style is called his *Blue Period.* When he fell in love with a neighbor, he painted happier pictures in shades of pink. This style is called his *Rose Period.* Then came his cubist period, and later he painted in a style that reminded viewers of Greek sculpture.

About the Media

Picasso created drawings, oil paintings, ceramic pieces, sculptures, prints, and engravings. He also invented collage along with the French artist Georges Braque. They combined colored papers, newspaper, old illustrations, and small objects with painting and drawing to produce collages.

About the Technique

In his cubist paintings, Picasso simplified his subjects into circles, triangles, and other basic shapes. He often outlined these shapes in black or a bright color.

Artist Profile

Horace Pippin
1888-1946

Horace Pippin (här´ əs pip´ ən) was an African American artist who painted historic figures and scenes from African American culture. He was born in West Chester, Pennsylvania, and grew up in Goshen, New York, where he attended a segregated elementary school. His first drawings were biblical scenes, and at the age of 14, he created his first portrait. He enlisted in the army in 1917, but returned to West Chester in the following year with a paralyzed right arm. After spending nine years in rehabilitation, Pippin regained enough strength and dexterity to continue painting. His first solo show was in West Chester in 1937. A year later he exhibited four of his paintings at a folk art exhibition at the Museum of Modern Art. By the mid-1940s, Pippin's works were on display in museums from Washington, D.C. to San Francisco.

About Art History

Naive art is artwork made by a person who has had little or no formal training. These artists, often known as *outsider artists*, invent their own conventions. Although many naive artists are self-taught, many others simply imitate other naive artists. Their art has a fresh, uncluttered style characterized by vibrant colors, defined shapes, and nonscientific perspectives. The absence of perspective often creates an illusion of figures floating in space. Naive art also has a childlike quality, which includes simple elements. Pippin's work is representative of naive art.

About the Artwork

Pippin tended to paint his subjects at the very front of his picture plane. In his 1945 painting *Victorian Parlor* he used simplified forms and bright colors to create the image of a traditional Victorian home's parlor. The lack of depth indicates his naive style and self-taught perspectives. The chairs appear to hover in the foreground of the piece and do not seem to be completely rooted to the floor. Pippin's subject matter includes scenes of contemporary life and the everyday experiences of African Americans.

About the Media

The majority of Pippin's works were painted with oils on canvas.

About the Technique

Pippin used bright, vibrant colors and a simple, almost childlike style. A combination of sketching and painting contributed to his final compositions.

Artist Profile

Man Ray
1890–1976

Man Ray (man rā) was born in Philadelphia. His given name was Emanuel Rabinovitch. After studying architecture and engineering, he turned to painting. Ray moved to Paris in 1920, and to support himself, he took photographs of friends' paintings and of French celebrities. In time, Ray combined photography and painting by placing objects on photosensitive paper. He called the resulting image a *Rayograph*. A Rayograph was a pattern of shadows and tones rather than a photograph. Ray and his wife moved back and forth between Paris and the United States several times. He continued to paint and try new techniques until his death at age 86.

About Art History

Ray and his friend Marcel Duchamp helped found the Dada movement in New York. This movement was named by opening a dictionary and choosing a word at random. Dadaist artists were critical of traditional painting styles and made fun of them. In fact, the Dadaist movement was actually a revolt against these artistic styles. Ray himself purposely tried to paint works not only unlike other artists,' but even unlike his own earlier paintings. After Ray moved to Paris, he joined the surrealist movement, which attempted to find new relationships between unlikely objects. For example, one of Ray's surrealistic paintings is a huge pair of lips resting against a sunset.

About the Artwork

Along with paintings and photography, Ray produced films and what he called *ready-mades*. Ready-mades were commercially made objects sold as art. One such object was an old-fashioned iron that was painted black. Man Ray attached metal tacks to the bottom with the points facing outward. He meant to surprise people with his odd combination of materials.

About the Media

Along with his paintings, Rayographs, and ready-mades, this artist painted on glass with an airbrush.

About the Technique

Man Ray was constantly experimenting with new painting and photography techniques. One of his photographs is altered to give a woman three sets of eyes.

Artist Profile

Frederic Remington
1861–1909

Frederic Remington (freˊ drik reˊ ming tən) was born in Canton, New York, in 1861. As a young boy he loved to draw cowboys, Native Americans, soldiers, and horses. When he was 19 years old, he left college and traveled west. He spent four years working as a cowboy and rancher, sketching constantly. When he returned to New York, he began to create illustrations of western life for popular magazines, bolstered by frequent trips out west in the following years. Remington became famous for his realistic portrayal of the American West, a subject that became the focus of his life's work.

▲ **Frederic Remington.** (American). *Self-Portrait on a Horse.* c. 1890.

Oil on canvas. $29\frac{3}{16} \times 19\frac{3}{8}$ inches. (74.14 cm × 49.21 cm.). Sid Richardson Collection of Western Art, Fort Worth, Texas.

About Art History

Remington was first noticed for his artwork in 1885 when American interest was directed to the West and westward expansion. Soon there was a great demand for his paintings and sculptures, which helped shape the romantic concept of the West that eventually made its way into cowboy movies. He claimed to be a self-taught artist, though his detailed style and clear narrative compositions suggest that he studied French academic art and artists such as Jean-Léon Gérôme.

About the Artwork

Remington drew and sculpted horses so realistically that he was credited as the first American to give "character" to the horse in art. Horses had previously been drawn in stiff-legged, static, posed positions that did not accurately capture their movements. The wild excitement and movement of his 1895 sculpture *The Bronco Buster* is one of his realistic, active depictions of horses. One of his most famous bronze sculptures, *Mountain Man*, helped generate the rugged, romantic vision of the West. It is a portrait depicting a man in America's western frontier, idealizing the pioneering spirit and individual determination typical of Remington's characters.

About the Media

Remington painted most of his paintings in oil on canvas, and he also created bronze sculptures.

About the Technique

Remington traveled west on specific sketching tours, drawing everything he saw and incorporating it into a composition when he returned to his studio at home. His experience as a cowboy, scout, and sheep rancher gave him substantial experience with frontier people and workers as well as all types of animals.

Artist Profile

Faith Ringgold
b. 1930

Faith Ringgold (fāth ring´gōld) grew up in Harlem in New York City. As a child her asthma often kept her home from school. To pass the time her mother taught her how to draw and sew. After high school Ringgold wanted to become an artist, but at the time the City College of New York did not allow women to study liberal arts. Instead Ringgold became an art teacher and taught for almost 20 years. She used her own artwork to draw attention to the challenges faced by African Americans, especially women.

About Art History

Ringgold has helped make African art popular in the United States. She has also promoted the use of fabric art.

About the Artwork

Ringgold focuses on the lives of African Americans. Her work ranges from cloth portraits of individuals to quilted squares that tell stories. By the 1980s, people had started to notice and admire Ringgold's work. Today she is a respected artist who is still finding new ways to express her feelings.

About the Media

At first Ringgold worked in oils, watercolors, and acrylics. Then a student suggested that Ringgold do what she taught her students to do: work with traditional African materials. Ringgold now creates life-sized cloth masks of people such as her aunts and the Reverend Martin Luther King Jr. The masks are attached to clothing and can be worn like costumes.

Ringgold also makes quilts and soft-sculpture people from stuffed stockings. Her quilts tell stories, with and without words. *Church Picnic,* for example, shows how a minister and a young woman fell in love. Sometimes Ringgold combines her quilts with singing and dancing to tell stories.

About the Technique

Ringgold uses bright colors and bold patterns to show the energy of the African American community.

Artist Profile

Diego Rivera
1886–1957

Diego Rivera (dē ā´ gō rē bā´ rä) was one of the most productive Mexican artists. He attended art school in Mexico but did not stay long. His first exhibition of paintings in 1907 won him a scholarship to Europe. There he studied the work of modern artists. After returning from a second trip to Europe in 1911, he became Mexico's leading mural painter. Rivera was a large man with strong opinions. His great love for his people and his country showed in his art. Crowds gathered to watch him paint his large murals on public walls. His third wife was the famous painter Frida Kahlo. They often fought and separated, but they always supported each other's artistic efforts.

About Art History

Rivera's painting style was influenced by the work of Klee, Cézanne, Picasso, and pre-Columbian, ancient Mexican art. He wanted to create art that could be enjoyed and understood by ordinary people. For this reason, Rivera focused on simple designs and interesting subjects. Public murals were ideal for him because many people could see his work.

About the Artwork

Rivera painted more than two-and-a-half miles of murals in Mexico, California, Michigan, and New York. For a huge stairway at the National Palace in Mexico City, Mexico, Rivera painted 124 panels. The panels trace the history of Mexico. In his other murals, Rivera often showed peasants working or celebrating.

About the Media

Rivera completed about 300 *frescoes*, which are paintings on fresh, moist plaster. He also painted on canvas with oils and watercolors.

About the Technique

For his frescoes, Rivera drew his designs on damp plaster and then copied them onto transparent paper. If the plaster dried out before Rivera could complete the painting, his assistant used the paper to re-create the designs on the wall.

Artist Profile

Henri Rousseau
1844–1910

Henri Rousseau (än rē´ rōō sō´) was born in a small town in France. When he was young he played the clarinet. He also spent some time in the French army. At the age of 25 he moved to Paris, where he spent most of his life. For a long time he worked as a customs clerk. He never went to art school. He learned to paint by practicing in gardens around the city.

◀ **Henri Rousseau.** (French). *Myself* (detail). 1890.

Oil on canvas. $57\frac{1}{2} \times 44\frac{1}{2}$ inches (146 × 113 cm.). National Gallery, Prague, Czech Republic.

About Art History

Because Rosseau had no formal art training, he is classified as a self-taught artist. The elements of fantasy and mystery in many of his paintings influenced the art movement of surrealism in the 1920s.

About the Artwork

Most of Rousseau's paintings look unlike anyone else's. In his first paintings he portrayed people and places around Paris. His most famous paintings are exotic portrayals of deserts and jungles. Many include wild animals, such as lions and monkeys. Rousseau often painted pictures of people from faraway countries. His paintings are known for their details. In some he painted every leaf on every tree and every whisker on every animal. Many of his paintings evoke the same feelings as strange dreams.

About the Media

Rousseau generally worked in oils on canvas. He mixed his colors well to make them look smooth.

About the Technique

Many people wondered where Rousseau got the ideas for his paintings. He told them that he had visited Mexico, but that was not true. He actually painted his jungle pictures by looking at the plants in the Paris botanical gardens. The animals were inspired by pictures he saw in books. He used dolls as models for people. Rousseau painted shapes very carefully to make his subjects look real.

Artist Profile

Shirley Russell
1886–1985

Shirley Russell (shûr´ lē rə´ səl) was born in California and studied art in college at Stanford University. The turning point in her career was a trip to Hawaii with her son after her husband died in 1921. Russell returned to Hawaii in 1923 and began a 23-year teaching career. Russell also studied art in Paris to build her creative skills from 1927 to 1928 and from 1937 to 1938. Her work has been exhibited not only in Hawaii, but also in Los Angeles, San Francisco, Cincinnati, New York City, and Baltimore. Her last show was held when she was 93.

About Art History

Like many Hawaiian artists, Russell painted the life around her. She said, "I am generally very happy when painting flowers." She might be considered part of the Hawaiian modern school of painting, which existed from 1894 to 1941. This group of artists, made up of some residents and some visitors, recorded their interpretations of Hawaii using modern painting styles.

About the Artwork

Russell concentrated on seascapes, landscapes, and still lifes. One of her well-known paintings is titled *Boys' Day*. It shows what was once an annual Hawaiian celebration held in plantation camps and in the Asian section of towns. The celebration featured long streamers of brightly colored paper carp hung from poles and rooftops. By swimming upstream, carp persist in the face of overwhelming odds. The village elders thought the carp offered a good model for young boys.

About the Media

This artist worked mainly in oils on canvas.

UNIT 3 • Lesson 1

Artist Profile

Pamela Spitzmueller

Pamela Spitzmueller (pâm´ ə lə spiz´ myū lər) is a respected book artist and conservator with a specialty in rare books and the history of book structures. Conservators study and preserve old books, often saving or unearthing history lessons while they work. She began studying bookbinding in 1976 with the renowned book conservator Gary Frost and has trained with conservators across the country and in Ireland for more than 25 years. She has lectured on many book history topics including aesthetics, ethics, book making, papermaking, and conservation. Since 1991, she has co-directed Paper and Book Intensive, a program that teaches students about the book arts.

▲ **Pamela Spitzmueller.** (American). *British Museum Memoir.* 1977.

Small grid graph paper, colored pencil, copper sheet, and copper wire. 11 × 47 inches (27.94 × 119.38 cm.). National Museum of Women in the Arts, Washington, D.C.

About Art History

Spitzmueller began her training at Chicago's Newberry Library, where she became the rare book conservator. She then became rare book conservator at the Library of Congress where she worked primarily on American, Hebraic, Islamic, and European books and manuscripts. Spitzmueller is now the chief conservator for special collections at the Harvard University and Harvard College Libraries.

About the Artwork

Spitzmueller was inspired to create her *British Museum Memoir* after a museum where fascinating objects were exhibited inside glass cases. These curious items were inviting to viewers but were never fully accessible because of their display cases. The many crumpled, textured pages of Spitzmueller's *British Museum Memoir* are like those tantalizing museum objects. They are bound between shiny copper covers that invite a viewer to come closer, but they never completely divulge the artist's secret and meaning.

About the Media

Spitzmueller uses numerous media for her work, including various papers, velvet, nuts and bolts, and thread.

About the Technique

Spitzmueller begins her books with one or more folded and gathered sheets of paper, which she then sews through the center fold or glues together at one edge. After the pages are joined, she attaches cover materials along the spine of the book.

Artist Profile

Wayne Thiebaud
b. 1920

Wayne Thiebaud (wān tē´ bō), one of California's most famous contemporary painters, has earned as many awards for excellence in teaching as he has for his painting and printmaking. He became interested in drawing in high school and later worked as a freelance cartoonist and illustrator. He continued his artwork during his military service in the U.S. Air Force during World War II. He drew cartoons for the military base newspaper. In 1949 Thiebaud decided to become a painter. His first one-person show in New York City was praised by the critics. At that time his subjects were mass-produced consumer goods, particularly junk food, and he was mistakenly classified with the pop artists. Later, he was classified as an American realist. His primary interest is organizing realistic subject matter into abstract compositions.

About Art History

Thiebaud arrived on the New York art scene in the 1960s when pop art was developing. He is sometimes identified as a pop artist because of the subject matter in much of his work. For example, many of his works show such objects as pinball machines, lipstick, and food. Thiebaud started as a realistic painter but later simplified his work, making it more abstract.

About the Artwork

Thiebaud reduces shapes to simple forms in his city landscapes. The viewer can easily identify circles, squares, triangles, rectangles, and arcs.

About the Media

Thiebaud paints with oils and acrylics, and creates a variety of prints.

About the Technique

Thiebaud tested mixing acrylic paint with oil paint, but he found that the mixture dissolved. He then tried painting oils over acrylics and discovered that he could achieve the effects he wanted. Before beginning to paint, Thiebaud stares at an object for a long time. Then he changes and adapts the object until it is the way he wants it in his painting.

• Artist Profile •

Joseph Turner
1775-1851

Regarded as one of the founders of English watercolor landscape painting, Joseph Mallord William Turner (jō´ sef ma´ lərd wil´ yəm tûr´ nər) was born in London, England. His father was a barber, his mother died when he was very young, and he received very little schooling as a child. Despite his lack of formal education, he was very interested in art and began his long artistic career by making drawings at home that he displayed in his father's barbershop window. Turner swiftly earned high praise and patronage, and he translated his landscape paintings into expressions of his own romantic feelings. As he grew older Turner lived with his father and became an eccentric, isolating himself from society.

About Art History

When Turner was only 15, one of his paintings was exhibited at the Royal Academy in London, and by the time he was 18 he had his own studio. While attending the Royal Academy Schools he studied with architectural draftsman and topographer Thomas Malton. After achieving a respected reputation he was elected as an associate of the Royal Academy and became a full member in 1802 at the young age of twenty-seven.

About the Artwork

Turner's earlier work featured somber, subdued colors but revealed his characteristic fascination with the contrasting effects of light and the atmospheric effects of storms and rainbows. He emulated the old masters at the turn of the century, but soon turned to his own personal themes, which extracted the essence of traditional styles while simultaneously taking them apart. His later style featured both the dreamlike idyllic landscapes inspired by his travels to Venice, Italy, and depictions of the destructiveness of nature. His seascapes often displayed this darker theme. Turner used open brushwork to create vortex-like compositions.

About the Media

Turner's work includes watercolors, oil paintings, and engravings. He focused on landscapes and included some figurative work later in his career.

About the Technique

When Turner moved from traditional styles to a more personal approach he made numerous pencil and watercolor sketches from nature. These studies served as references for his paintings and also as a means of financial security, so he could complete paintings that diverged from contemporary taste. Turner made sketches with the intention of using them later, and sometimes they sat in his studio for years before he incorporated them into finished compositions.

UNIT 2 • Lesson 2

Artist Profile

Vaclav Vytlacil
1892–1984

Although he was born in New York, Vaclav Vytlacil (vä klev vət´ la sil) grew up in the Midwest. He took classes at the Art Institute of Chicago as a child and moved back to New York City in 1913 to attend the Art Students League. He taught at the Minneapolis School of Art. After saving some money, Vytlacil traveled and studied art in Europe. In Munich he met Hans Hofmann, a painter who became his mentor. Vytlacil left Europe to give a series of lectures at the University of California at Berkeley before joining the faculty of the Art Students League. After spending more time abroad, Vytlacil helped found the American Abstract Artists and taught at a variety of schools, including Queens College in New York and Black Mountain College in North Carolina.

About Art History

When Vaclav Vytlacil met Hofmann, he began to rethink his own art. Hofmann helped develop *abstract expressionism*—a style that emphasizes spontaneous yet often carefully planned paintings that show emotions. Vytlacil was intrigued by the revolutionary modern art ideas circulating through Europe. When he returned to America, he was influenced by other visionaries in New York, such as Jackson Pollock and Arshile Gorky.

About the Artwork

Vytlacil, following the instruction of Hofmann, spent much time in Europe focusing on drawn forms. He believed that a painter must first learn to draw. Later Vytlacil created paintings, especially landscapes, that fused an expressionistic use of color with forms that are broken and put back together.

About the Media

Although Vytlacil experimented with three-dimensional wooden and cardboard constructions, he primarily created charcoal drawings and paintings using oils or tempera paints.

About the Technique

Vytalcil's paintings show an interest in form and color rather than in realism. Gradually he began to focus more on energy than on form, and his late paintings were full of freedom and movement.

Artist Profile

Andy Warhol
1928–1987

Andy Warhol (an´ dē wôr´ hôl) was born Andrew Warhola in Pittsburgh, Pennsylvania. After graduating from the Carnegie Institute of Technology, he moved to New York and became a successful commercial artist and illustrator. Fascinated with consumer culture, the media, and fame, his photography and silkscreen paintings were often critiqued as both an ingenious expression of American culture or a base representation of low, common imagery.

About Art History

During the 1950s, Warhol's drawings were published in magazines and department stores, and he became known for his illustrations of I. Miller shoes. By the 1960s he began to paint comic strip characters and images from advertisements, as seen in his 1962 painting *Campbell's Soup Cans.* He also began painting celebrities and produced series of subjects, including flowers, Marilyn Monroe, Elvis, and household products. In 1963 the artist substituted a silkscreen process for painting by hand. The 1970s saw Warhol create more celebrity portraits, and he returned to the gestural brushwork of his earlier career. He also became interested in writing and published his autobiography *The Philosophy of Andy Warhol* in 1975.

About the Artwork

Warhol saw his work as a link with contemporary mass culture. His use of repetition mimicked the practice of mass advertising. He also painted celebrity portraits and addressed issues of disaster and death in his silkscreen creations.

About the Media

The silkscreen process involves photomechanical reproduction techniques which use photographs to create an image. Its ability to replicate imagery allowed Warhol to explore his theme of repetition and to transfer multiple images onto a single canvas. By repeating imagery of a subject, Warhol succeeded in distancing his viewers from the subject and encouraging them to think about the way contemporary culture saturates itself with information and visual stimulation.

About the Technique

Warhol used photography to capture an image of his subjects and often used commercial photos from advertisements and magazines for references. Photo-silkscreen allowed him to enlarge and transfer an image onto canvas, which he would then paint with flat patches of color to give the composition energy and uniqueness.

Artist Profile

Idelle Weber
b. 1932

Born in Chicago, Idelle Weber (i del´ we´ bər) grew up in Wilmette, Illinois, and Los Angeles, California. Drawing was her passion from an early age, and at the age of eight she became the youngest student to attend the Chouinard Art Institute of Los Angeles. Weber then moved to New York and painted images of city life in an abstract style. She was always fascinated with how things worked and were made and was very interested in depicting the lifestyles and objects she encountered while living in New York City.

About Art History
Weber graduated from the University of California at Los Angeles with a master of fine arts degree in 1955. In the 1960s, she became one of the few female artists to join the pop art movement, and she abandoned her earlier abstract work for photorealism. She began teaching in 1974 and has been a professor at Harvard, New York University, and Long Island University in New York.

About the Artwork
Weber's later photorealistic paintings depict figure silhouettes in offices, grocery stores, and hotel lobbies, and were meant to articulate a human loneliness. She also paints still lifes of city objects such as fruit stands, pushcarts, and garbage on the streets, and she uses her garbage paintings to comment on the lifestyle differences between New York's wealthy elite and its lower-class poor. Color and form are important to her compositions, and she often uses a bright palette. In *Pistia Kew,* for example, Weber's focus on color and form is shown, and her attention to detail and realism cause the viewer to wonder if her painting is actually a photograph.

About the Media
Weber's work is sketched in pencil or charcoal on linen canvas. Linen is a finely woven fabric and provides a smooth surface for the artist's oil paints. In addition to her photorealistic paintings, Weber has also worked in printmaking.

About the Technique
Photorealists create paintings that look like photographs. Weber first takes a photograph of her subject and then plots a grid over it. She then draws a matching grid onto her canvas that allows her to accurately sketch a copy of the gridded photo. Once her drawing is complete she fills it in with oil paints. Sometimes she chooses to use colors in her paintings that were not in the original photographs.

Artist Profile

William T. Wiley
b. 1937

William T. Wiley (wil´ yəm wī´ lē) was born in Indiana, but has lived mostly in California. He earned two degrees from the San Francisco Art Institute. He has taught at art schools and universities across the nation, but he says that his students have taught him more than he has taught them. Wiley is married and has a son.

About Art History

In 1967, Wiley made an important discovery. He realized that he could create art any way he wanted and did not have to worry about pleasing art critics. He now has his own style, which borrows from pop art by focusing on common objects. It also borrows from surrealism by placing these objects in unexpected settings. Wiley's style is a form of abstract art that combines objects with personal symbols. Wiley was one of the first artists to include verbal humor in his art. He uses misspelled words and double meanings to express his opinion. For example, across one painting he wrote, "These guise will fry anything."

About the Artwork

Wiley has explored the nature of art and the role of the artist. His work ranges from realistic landscapes to nearly abstract paintings. Some of his paintings look like children's games or strange maps. His recent paintings tend to be darker and moodier than his earlier ones. They give the sense that a terrible event is about to happen.

About the Media

Wiley creates oil paintings, watercolors, wash-and-ink drawings, murals, sculpture, and prints. Sometimes he adds feathers, strings, sticks, or ropes to his works.

About the Technique

Wiley sometimes places childish things in adult settings. For example, he might show a coloring book or comic book in a landscape painting. He also makes real objects look unreal. Wiley often writes words, sentences, and even short poems over his paintings of images and symbols.

Artist Profile

Nancy Youngblood
b. 1955

Nancy Youngblood was born in Fort Lewis, Washington. Her mother is Native American, and her father is of British descent. Her father was in the military, so they moved many times. She has lived on and off in Santa Clara, New Mexico. At a very early age, she wanted to be an artist. She went to the San Franciso Art Institute on a scholarship. Later, she worked in an art gallery, which featured Native American works. The owner, Al Packard, encouraged her to follow in her family's footsteps. She had her first major show when she was 20. Youngblood still lives in Santa Clara and has three sons. She says that each work, which she never rushes to finish, surprises and challenges her.

About Art History

Southwestern potters have been using the same type of clay and methods for centuries. Youngblood is part of a long tradition of well-known potters from the Tafoya family. Her grandmother was Margaret Tafoya.

About the Artwork

Although Youngblood has continued to use traditional southwestern Native American styles in her work, she manages to make each piece distinctly hers. She continues to incorporate the traditional black matte finish, and incorporates designs like seashells into surfaces made of caramel-colored slip. All show the natural, rich colors of the earth.

About the Media

Youngblood digs clay from the hills around Santa Clara. She prepares the clay through a long, painstaking process that can take several months.

About the Technique

Youngblood rolls clay in long coils, then winds these coils until they form a pot. With her fingers, she smears the coils into each other to form the sides of the pot. When the pot feels hard but not too dry, she starts carving. Then the pot needs to finish drying. This can take up to ten months. Youngblood puts the pot into a bag for a few hours a day so that it will not dry too quickly. After this stage, she sands the pot with sandpaper. Later, she applies colored slip and then smooth stone. She fires her pots individually at the Pueblo reservation where she built a firing shed.

Artist Profile

Child's Beaded Shirt

Most native Plains women made clothing for members of their families. Their designs were usually abstract and geometric. The patterns in these designs were often balanced. This shirt was probably made by an individual of the northern Cheyenne or Teton Dakota culture.

▲ **Artist unknown.** (Northern Cheyenne or Teton Dakota/United States). *Child's Beaded Shirt.* c. 1865.

Buffalo hide, glass seed beads. $13\frac{3}{16} \times 23$ inches (33.5 × 58.5 cm.). Dallas Museum of Art, Dallas, Texas.

About Art History

Before their contact with nonnatives, Plains people decorated much of their clothing with paint and porcupine quill embroidery. They were fascinated with the beads they discovered through trade. The earliest beads were large and were called *pony beads* because traders brought them west in pony pack trains. By the 1850s Plains people had access to smaller beads called *seed beads*. After the Civil War many styles of beadwork developed. The golden age of Native American beadwork began in the 1880s. By this time women had more time to devote to beadwork as an art form and more colors of beads to use. The women also added European designs and patterns to their handiwork.

About the Artwork

The artist used red, white, and blue beads in this child's shirt. The designs on the shirt were common in the central Plains area. Balance was created by repeating shapes and lines, in the same colors, down each side and on the sleeves of the shirt.

About the Media

Glass seed beads were stitched onto a buffalo hide to create this shirt.

About the Technique

Two basic techniques were used to stitch beads to skins. The first stitch is known as the *spot* or *overlay* stitch. Artists threaded beads on a sinew. With a second sinew they sewed the beaded sinew onto the skin by stitching between every second or third bead. The second stitch is called the *lazy stitch*. With this method beads were threaded onto a sinew and only the ends of the sinew were attached to the skin. The first method produces a smooth surface; the second method produces a rougher surface.

Artist Profile

Artist unknown. (Mojave, United States). *Collar.* 1900–1925.

Glass beads and threads.
Birmingham Museum of Art, Birmingham, Alabama.

Collar

This beaded collar was made by an unknown artist of the Mojave from the southwestern United States. The Mojave are native to the Mojave Desert area and have adapted their lifestyle to its hot, dry environment. The Mojave were able to make many of the things needed for survival from a single kind of tree, the mesquite. They used the wood, bark, and leaves to build their homes, the bark to make clothing and tea, and even ate the seed pods and flowers of the trees. Before 1600, the Mojave were the largest ethnic group living in southwestern North America.

About Art History

Before contact with nonnative peoples, Native American artists decorated their clothing with paint and porcupine quill embroidery. Afterward, Native Americans were fascinated with the beads they discovered through trade. The earliest beads were large and were called *pony beads*. By the 1850s Native Americans also had access to much smaller beads. The tiniest beads were called *seed beads*, named for their resemblance to plant seeds. The beadwork on this collar was done with small seed beads.

About the Artwork

The pattern on this beaded collar was made by stitching tiny white, blue, yellow, red, and black beads to a base cloth. The long fringe along the bottom of the collar was made by stringing beads onto flexible strands of thread or rawhide.

About the Media

This collar was made from cloth and small glass beads in various colors.

About the Technique

Two basic techniques were used to stitch beads to cloth and animal hides. The first technique was known as the *spot* or *overlay* stitch. Artists threaded the beads onto a *sinew*, a semiflexible needle made from the tendon of an animal. With a second sinew they sewed the beaded sinew onto the cloth or hide by stitching between every second or third bead. The second stitch technique was called *the lazy stitch*. For this stitch, beads were threaded onto a sinew and only the ends of the sinew were attached to the cloth or hide. The spot stitch produces a smooth surface; the lazy stitch produces a rougher surface.

Artist Profile

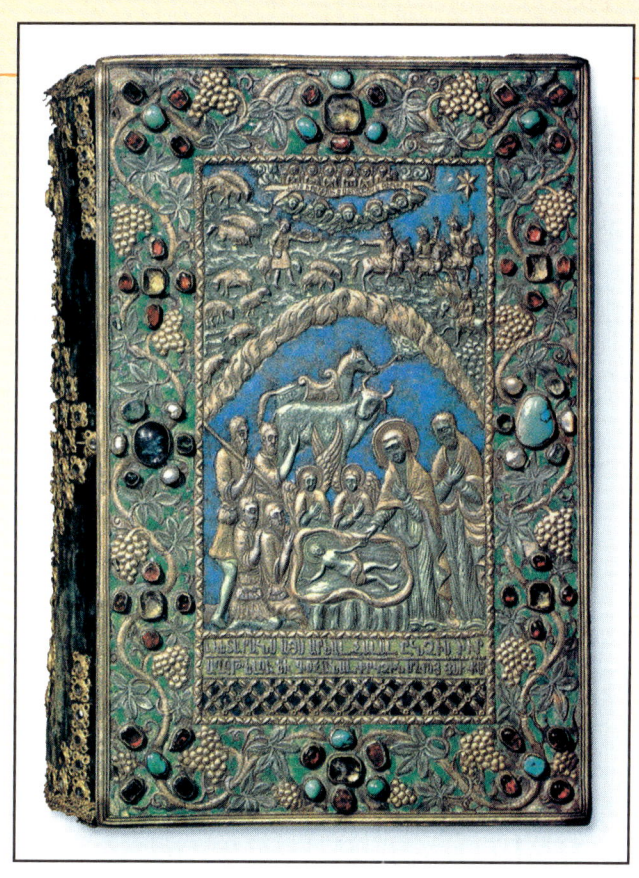

Cover of an Armenian Book

This cover was made in 1691 in the Armenian city of Kayseri, Turkey, the home of skilled silversmiths and goldsmiths. The illustrations inside were completed by artists from the city of Cicilia who were known for their painting skills. The words in the book were written by a scribe named Gregor. He gilded some letters in the first part of the book.

◀ **Artist Unknown.** (Armenia). *Cover of Armenian Book.* Thirteenth century.

Carved and hammered silver, gilded and enameled, and set with jewels and rubricated vellum. $10\frac{1}{4} \times 7\frac{3}{8}$ inches (26.04 x 18.73 cm.). The Metropolitan Museum of Art, New York, New York.

About Art History

Christianity became the official religion of Armenia during the fourth century. At that time the traditional art of Armenia began to disappear as a new kind of art became popular. Armenian artists used scenes from the Gospels and images of Christianity to decorate their churches and to illustrate their manuscripts. Existing illustrated Armenian manuscripts date from the ninth to the seventeenth centuries. They are based on early Christian and Byzantine art but tend to be more lively and dramatic.

About the Artwork

This book contains floral, geometric, and animal motifs. The center panel shows shepherds worshipping the Christ child and the Magi following the star. The back cover shows Christ's resurrection, including a tomb with a sleeping guard and two standing soldiers.

About the Media

This book cover was created from silver and semiprecious stones.

About the Technique

The cover was engraved in silver. The grapevine in the design has a green enamel background and contains precious and semiprecious stones. The spine of the cover is also decorated with semiprecious jewels.

Artist Profile

Covered Jar

This covered jar was probably made by a professional artist trained in the craft of pottery. Many excellent potters lived in China during the Ming dynasty. They produced many beautiful jars like this one.

◀ **Artist unknown.** (China). *Covered Jar.* 1522–1566.
Porcelain painted with underglaze cobalt blue and overglaze enamels. $18\frac{1}{2}$ inches (47 cm.) high, $15\frac{3}{4}$ inches (40 cm.) diameter. Asia Society of New York, New York.

About Art History

This jar was made during the Ming dynasty. The term *dynasty* refers to a series of rulers who come from the same family and rule a country for a long time. The Ming dynasty spanned from 1368 to 1644. Many great works of art, such as porcelain and silk items, were produced during this time. These items were exported by boat to faraway places like Africa and Europe.

About the Artwork

This Ming dynasty jar is painted with many designs and details. The designs around the *base* (bottom) and *shoulder* (rounded top below the lid) of the jar were used on many Ming jars. The underwater scene of catfish, seaweed, and floating leaves was typical of scenes depicted on jars from the Ming dynasty. Porcelain jars like this one are very thin and delicate.

About the Media

This covered jar is made of porcelain. Porcelain is made by baking a fine white clay called *kaolin*. Paint was used to color the designs.

About the Technique

Jars like this one are made from lumps of soft, wet clay. The clay is put on a flat, spinning wheel and then shaped by the artist's hands as it spins. When the artist is pleased with how it looks, the wheel is stopped and the jar set out to dry. Some of the designs on the jar were made by laying thin layers of clay over the jar's surface. Then designs were cut into this thin layer. The jar was baked in a very hot oven to make it harden. The heat burned the designs into the jar in the places where the thin layer of clay was cut. The finished jar was painted with cobalt blue, and glazed with enamels.

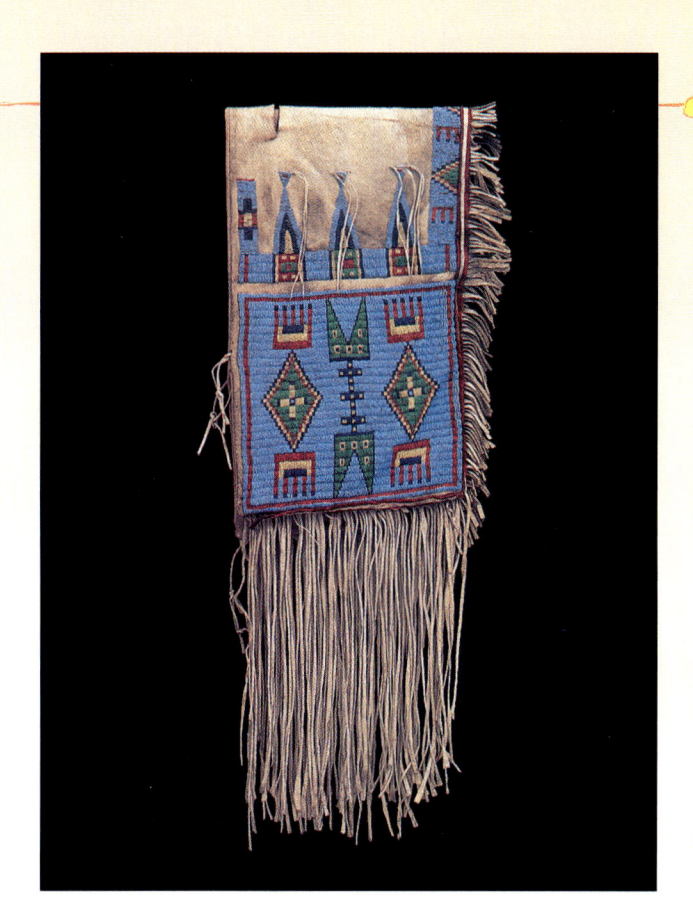

Artist Profile

Double Saddlebag

The Sioux were native to the northern plains of North America, including land now known as Minnesota, the Dakotas, and Nebraska. They hunted their food and followed migrating herds of buffalo across the plains. During the mid-1800s, settlers and gold seekers killed many buffalo on the Sioux hunting reservations. Although groups led by Sitting Bull and Crazy Horse fought back, the Sioux eventually lost their freedom to choose where they lived. Now about half of the existing Sioux live on reservations. The others live in cities across the United States, where many work to preserve Sioux traditions and crafts.

◀ **Artist unknown (Native American, Sioux).** (United States). *Double Saddlebag.* 1875.

Buckskin, canvas, glass beads, sinew, and wool. 45 × 13 inches (113.7 × 33 cm.). Detroit Institute of Arts, Detroit, Michigan.

About the Artwork

A double saddlebag was placed over a horse's back behind the rider. The pockets on each side could hold the rider's food and other supplies. The Sioux used their highly decorated clothing and saddlebags only for ceremonies and other special occasions.

About the Media

Common materials for Sioux saddlebags included buckskin (deerskin), canvas, porcupine quills or glass beads, sinew thread made from animal tendons, and wool.

About the Technique

Long ago, Sioux women made beads by cutting dyed porcupine quills. Some artists still use these kinds of beads. Later, many of the women traded with the Europeans for glass beads. They sewed beads onto their saddlebags and clothing in short rows to produce geometric designs. The symbolic meanings of these designs were not always the same for the maker and the wearer.

Artist Profile

Easy Chair

Caleb Gardner is the artist credited with making this easy chair in the city of Newport, Rhode Island, in 1758. Very little has been documented about this individual and his work, but it is known that Gardner died in 1761. This easy chair has been carefully preserved and the condition of the fabric and wood are excellent for an antique from this time period.

◀ **Caleb Gardner.** (American). *Easy Chair.* 1758.

Walnut, maple, and hand-stitched upholstery.
$46\frac{3}{8} \times 32\frac{3}{8} \times 25\frac{7}{8}$ inches (117.8 × 82.2 × 65.7 cm.).
The Metropolitan Museum of Art. New York, New York.

About Art History

The style of this chair is typical of easy chairs made in America during the mid-eighteenth century. It is wide, high-backed, and heavily padded with down filler. The "wings" to the sides of the headrest provide a buffer against cold drafts. This type of easy chair would have been used in a bedroom or living area, probably positioned facing a fire during colder months. Although the style of the chair is common, what makes it unique and exceptionally beautiful is the pattern and stitch work of the upholstery.

About the Artwork

The frame of the chair is inscribed with the words "Gardner Junr" and "Newport, May 1758." This suggests that Gardner may have done the upholstery work on the chair or may have been the artist who constructed, covered, and decorated the entire piece. It is not known what other types of artwork or furniture Gardner created.

About the Media

This easy chair is made from the wood of maple and walnut trees. The chair is covered in cloth upholstery, silk tape, and embroidery thread.

About the Technique

This easy chair was constructed from wood, and then covered with heavy upholstery fabric. The fabric was decorated with Irish-stitch needlework, and the back of the chair was covered with a wonderfully detailed and colorful landscape scene. The chair's seams were concealed beneath ribbons of silk tape.

Artist Profile

Hat: Birds and Geometric Patterns

In the region now known as Peru, in the Andes Mountains of South America, the Incan empire slowly replaced an even older culture, the Wari. The ancient Incan empire had no coins or dollar bills. Handwoven cloth and clothing had so much value that they were often used in place of money. The Incas also had another use for clothing. Like the ancient Egyptians, they wanted to preserve the bodies of people who had died. They often wrapped the dead in clothing and placed hats on their heads. Some ancient mummies have been found wrapped in dozens of layers of handwoven cloth.

▲ **Artist unknown.** (Peru). *Hat: Birds and Geometric Patterns.* 700–1000 A.D.

Alpaca and cotton. $4\frac{1}{2} \times 5$ inches (11 × 13 cm.).
The Seattle Art Museum. Seattle, Washington.

About Art History

The Wari, and the Inca after them, decorated their clothing and other objects with images of animals and geometric designs that represented ancient myths and wars. When the Spaniards invaded the Incan empire in the fifteenth century, they took advantage of the Incas' artistic skills. However, they wanted the Inca to use Spanish designs in their work. Some of the containers produced during this period have geometric patterns on one section and Spanish floral designs on another.

About the Artwork

The designs on ancient Wari and Incan hats and other clothing probably had religious meaning, but this meaning has been lost over the centuries. The patterns, colors, and richness of the weaving also indicated the wearer's status.

About the Media

Incan craftspeople created clothing and hats from wool, cotton, or a combination of both.

About the Technique

The Inca wove designs into cloth, but did not embroider it. In later periods, the Spanish introduced embroidery so that Incan artists could decorate religious garments. Today Peruvian craftspeople sometimes use machine embroidery to add the same designs that ancient artists wove into garments.

Artist Profile

Hunting Scene on Handle from a Large Bowl

This beautiful work was created by an unknown Roman artist sometime during the second century A.D. or later. The portion shown here is just one part of the ornate decoration on a large bowl.

▲ **Artist unknown.** (Roman).
Hunting Scene on Handle from a Large Bowl.
Second century or later.

Silver. 5 × 14 3/8 × 35 inches (13 × 38 × 89 cm.).
The Metropolitan Museum of Art.

About Art History

Relief sculptures and portrait busts of Roman rulers were a popular art form during the late Empire and throughout much of ancient Roman history. It was important to Romans to have their images sculpted in the most flattering manner possible, and artists of this period were eager to please rulers by emphasizing their beauty, diminishing imperfections, and generally idealizing physical features. This trend, more typical of the artistic styles of classical Greece, may have been influenced by an interest in Greek art by Hadrian, emperor of Rome during the second century A.D.

About the Artwork

Very little is known about this particular piece. It can be assumed that it was made to honor the Roman ruler at the time it was made. Many works of Roman art displayed images that were meant to celebrate the strength, bravery, or athletic skill of members of the imperial family. In the scene shown in this detail, a hunter on horseback charges toward a crouching lion while other animals flee, perhaps suggesting that the bravery of this hunter was so great that he could face and defeat the most dangerous wild beast.

About the Media

This bowl handle was created in silver. Gilding appears on many of the raised portions of the relief.

Artist Profile

Jar

The artist who made this jar is unknown. The artist probably worked in one of the large ceramics factories located in Tz'u-hien, a province of Hopei in northeastern China.

◀ **Artist unknown.** (China). *Jar.*
Northern Song Period, twelfth century.

Stoneware with graffito design in slip under glaze.
12½ inches (31.75 cm.).
The Asia Society, New York, New York.

About Art History

This jar was made during the Northern Song dynasty. The Northern Song dynasty lasted from 960 to 1279 A.D. There were many different types of pottery made during the Northern Song period. This jar is of the Tz'u-chou type; it was named after the factory where it was made.

About the Artwork

The Tz'u-hien ceramics factory was famous for the special black-and-white decorative style seen on this jar. The technique used to create this ornate style is called *graffito*. This jar was probably a decorative object in a home or palace.

About the Media

This jar is made of porcelain. It is painted with white and black slip. *Slip* is a form of clay that is watered down and used as a coating.

About the Technique

This jar was made using a potter's wheel. The potter placed a lump of porcelain clay onto the flat, spinning disc, then pulled the clay into the shape of a jar. The jar was then removed from the wheel and dried. When it was dry it was decorated using the graffito technique. The first step was to cover the jar with white slip. When the white slip dried, black slip was painted on in ornamental designs. Then the artist carved details into the black slip with a thin knife. The jar was baked in a hot oven called a *kiln*.

UNIT 4 • Lesson 1

Artist Profile

Jar

The artist of this piece is unknown. The jar was made during the Middle Jomon period of Japanese history. During this period daily life consisted of hunting, gathering roots and berries, fishing, and collecting shellfish. The Jomon created a great number of ceramics in a wide variety of styles.

◀ **Artist unknown.** (Japan). *Jar.* c. 3000–2000 B.C.

Earthenware clay with applied, incised, and cord-marked decoration. $27\frac{1}{2}$ inches (69.85 cm.) high. The Metropolitan Museum of Art, New York, New York.

About Art History

The earliest Jomon pottery was created before 10,000 B.C. It is the oldest known pottery in the world. Ancient ceramics show how society changes over the centuries. Archaeologists study the shape, texture, method of manufacture, and location of pottery to learn about changes in food preparation, ceremonies, politics, and religious beliefs of a society. During the Middle Jomon period, new forms of ceramics, such as hanging lamps and pots with raised feet, were created. Some new shapes included shells and fish.

About the Artwork

The effects of the Jomon texturing process are stunning. Many pieces of this period feature overhanging rims or flared rims with pieces that stick out. Another common feature of this period is the use of raised bands to define the shoulder area of a piece. Middle Jomon ceramics may have been used for preparing, serving, eating, drinking, and storing food and drink.

About the Media

This jar was created out of clay and decorated using cord. Open fire as opposed to a kiln, was used to fire the finished jar.

About the Technique

Middle Jomon ceramics were handmade with clay coils. The surfaces were decorated when the clay was as hard as leather. The decorations were made with twisted cords or cord-wrapped sticks, which were pressed into the clay. Sometimes cords were intertwined and rolled over the surface to create an interesting texture. Multiple cords, knotted or applied in different directions, made a great variety of decorations. After decorations were added, the pots were fired in open bonfires.

Artist Profile

Mask with Seal or Sea Otter Spirit

This mask was made by an unidentified artist of the Yupik people who live in the Yukon River area, in what is today the state of Alaska. It is believed that the mask was made during the late nineteenth century. The subject of this mask is typical for artwork produced by the Yupik people. Many Yupik share the belief that everything in the natural world, including humans, animals, mountains, and even storms, has a soul or spirit. In some groups this spirit is known by the term *inua*. The smiling face in the center of the mask may represent the spirit of the sea otter or seal.

◀ **Artist unknown.** (American). *Mask with Seal or Sea Otter Spirit.* Nineteenth century.

Wood, paint, gut cord, and feathers.
$23\frac{1}{2} \times 22\frac{1}{4}$ inches (59.69 × 56.52 cm.).
Dallas Museum of Art, Dallas, Texas.

About Art History

The Yupik have an important relationship with animals and the natural world around them. Because they live by hunting, fishing, and making tools, clothing, and shelters from what is available in their environment, the lives of the Yupik people depend upon animals. This dependence has created a deep respect for these animals, and their likenesses are often included in Yupik works of art.

About the Artwork

This mask may have been used by a Yupik spiritual figure called a *shaman*. Shamans are believed to have the ability to pass between the material world of the living and the spirit world. One of the duties of a shaman in a Yupik community was to commune with the spirit world and ask for help in times of illness or famine. If a period of time came when there were too few game animals, making the hunting poor and food scarce, a shaman would ask certain spirits to send more animals to the material world. This mask may have been used by the shaman to show respect to the seal or otter spirit and also as a tribute to the harmony between humans and animals.

About the Media

This mask is made of wood, feathers, animal gut cord, and paint.

About the Technique

This mask appears to have been hand carved and hand painted. The feathers may have been affixed to the mask by fitting them into holes drilled or bored into the wood portion of the mask.

Artist Profile

Mihrab

Mihrabs are *niches,* or semicircular hollows, set into the middle of a qibla wall. The *qibla* wall is where people go to pray. It is not known who built this particular mihrab. Mihrabs were built by skilled craftspeople. Typically the structure was built by one group of workers, and the mosaic tiling was done by a separate group.

◀ **Artist unknown** (Iran). *Mihrab.* 1354.
Faience mosaic of glazed terra-cotta cut and embedded in plaster.
11 feet 3 inches × 7 feet 6 inches (3.4 × 2.3 meters).
The Metropolitan Museum of Art, New York, New York.

About Art History

The qibla wall is built outside a mosque, an Islamic communal house of prayer. The mihrab's purpose is to point the way to Mecca, the blessed city of the Islamic region. Before mihrabs were built, travelers were guided by a painted mark or a tree stump pointing the direction to Mecca. The first concave, hollowed-out mihrab was built in the Prophet's Mosque at Medina. Early mosques were built without mihrabs. Throughout history mihrab decoration became more complicated, and mihrabs were decorated in the latest artistic styles. The most recent mosques, such as the one in the city of Bengal, have several mihrabs set in the qibla wall.

About the Artwork

This mihrab, unlike most others, is from a school. But, like most mihrabs, it has no figurative images. This means that there are no images of people, animals, or other living beings on the mihrab. Geometric and floral shapes are the most common images found on mihrabs.

About the Media

The mihrab's surface is made of glazed terra-cotta. Terra-cotta is a kind of clay.

About the Technique

The colors and designs on this mihrab were made with terra-cotta tiles in a process called *mosaic.* Mosaic is similar to doing a puzzle: small pieces join together to form a bigger picture. Each piece of terra-cotta was individually glazed with color. Then, the pieces were arranged to create the larger image on the mihrab.

UNIT 1 • Lesson 4

Artist Profile

Necklace

This necklace was made by an unknown Berber artist in the Rif region of Morocco. The Berbers of North Africa live in the rugged Atlas, Rif, and Kabylia Mountains and the arid lands at the edge of the Sahara Desert. Berbers create art that is more Islamic than African in nature. As late as the fifteenth century, Jewish goldsmiths and silversmiths fleeing the Spanish Inquisition settled in northern Africa and introduced the jewelry-making techniques that are still used in the region.

▲ **Artist unknown.** (Morocco). *Necklace.* Twentieth century.

Beads and silver alloy. 14 inches (35.5 cm.) long. Private collection.

About Art History

Perhaps as a reaction to their difficult living environments in the mountains and desert, Berber women wore enormous amounts of colorful beads. Berber women believed that the beads provided the spiritual protection associated with coral and amber and the Koran, Islam's holy book. Beads were also a form of currency. The worth of the bead was often based on its weight, especially if it was made of silver. Silversmiths often melted down beads and reworked them because some Berbers preferred new beads to those worn by someone else.

About the Artwork

This necklace was part of a ceremonial dowry piece. The silver Koranic boxes are hollow and decorated with more silver. By including five of these boxes on the necklace, the artist made a powerful statement. The number five is an important number to Moroccans. It symbolizes the *khamsa*, which is believed to ward off evil forces. Muslims consider mathematics an integral part of art.

About the Media

This necklace features coral beads and silver coins on silver wire. Five silver Koranic boxes have been worked into the piece.

About the Technique

The coral beads on the necklace are strung onto three strands of silver wire. The Koranic boxes are interspersed geometrically throughout the piece. Each silver coin is attached to its own silver wire and is then connected to the bottom strand of the necklace. A Koranic box is made first by heating the silver, and then flattening it with a hammer before cutting it to the desired size. Then it is secured to a slab of wood where it can be inlaid with enamel or decorated with stones.

Artist Profile

Necklace

The artist, or goldsmith, who created this necklace was a member of the Baule culture of Côte d'Ivoire, formerly called the Ivory Coast, West Africa. The Baule people are one of the largest ethnic groups in the country of Côte d'Ivoire, numbering more than one million individuals, and they have maintained their cultural traditions to the present day. The culture of the Baule people is influenced by their belief that every person lived in a spirit world before being born, and thus everyone is influenced in this life by spirits and the supernatural. The majority of Baule people live in small fishing or farming villages.

◂ **Artist unknown.** (Ivory Coast). *Cote d' Ivoire.* c. 1900.

Gold. $118\frac{1}{2}$ inches (300 cm.). Museum of Fine Arts, Houston, Texas.

About Art History

Baule artists have created many works that have distinguished their culture as producers of some of Africa's most widely known and appreciated art. In Baule culture, specific types of artwork are made by men and others by women. For example, women have traditionally been the potters in Baule society, and men carve wood, cast metal, and weave cloth.

About the Artwork

Art historians specializing in African art can easily distinguish Baule gold jewelry from that of other west African cultures, most notably because of the unique rectangular and circular Baule pendants and beads. The rectangular beads displayed on this necklace indicate that it was made for a Baule chief. These beads, made to resemble doors, symbolize the chief's power to see all that is within the doors of his village and all that is beyond those doors in the outside world. The circular pendants represent the wealth passed down through the generations of the Baule chief's family.

About the Media

This necklace was made from solid gold. Gold can be found in rivers, streams, and fields throughout western Africa, and it is used in the creation of magnificent works of art symbolic of the power and prestige of African royalty.

About the Technique

The gold beads and pendants were carved, etched with fine detail, and finished before they were arranged and strung on the necklace cord. The type of material used to make the cord is unknown, but it is likely made of strong leather or plant fiber.

UNIT 2 • Lesson 6

Artist Profile

Portrait of a Boy

The Egyptian artist of this painting remains unknown. *Portrait of a Boy* is an example of Fayum portraits, named for the area where most of these paintings have been found. Although the portrait resembles paintings of the Roman tradition, the funerary purpose and iconography reflect the Egyptian culture.

◀ **Artist unknown.** (Egypt). *Portrait of a Boy.* Second century.

$15\frac{3}{8} \times 7\frac{1}{2}$ inches (39 × 19 cm.).
The Metropolitan Museum of Art, New York.

About Art History

In 30 B.C. the Romans took control of Egypt and for a while they continued the Egyptian tradition of burying the dead in mummy cases. During this period Egyptian drawings became more realistic and lifelike because of Greek and Roman influences. By the fourth century, bodies were buried in graves, without mummy cases or portraits.

About the Artwork

Roman portraits differed greatly from the flat, stiff drawings of the ancient Egyptians. The use of highlights and shading gave depth and personality to the portraits. The faces were often shown at a slight angle instead of in profile, or with the eyes staring directly and blankly at the viewer.

About the Media

This work was painted with *encaustic* paint. This kind of paint is made of pigments suspended in a wax medium. The wax is heated to a semi-liquid state and then applied to the surface.

About the Technique

The paints were made by mixing dry pigments with molten, white, refined beeswax and a small amount of resin from a warm palette. The manipulation of the paint by brush or palette knife was assisted by warming and chilling the surface. A final heat treatment was done by passing a heat source over the surface. This fused the painting and bonded it in its permanent form without altering it. A gentle polishing with soft cotton brought out a dull, satiny sheen. When cool, the picture was finished.

Artist Profile

Presentation of Captives to a Maya Ruler

The Mayan people—founders of a vast, powerful, and ancient kingdom—have historically lived throughout an enormous geographic area of what is today Mexico and Central America. Historians can date evidence of the Mayan culture back to 700 B.C. Mayan civilization had a complex written language, sophisticated methods of producing crops, accurate calendars and other methods of keeping time, and an impressive knowledge of astronomy.

◀ **Artist unknown.** (Mayan). *Presentation of Captives to a Maya Ruler.* c.785.

Limestone with traces of paint. $45\frac{3}{8} \times 35$ inches (114 × 89 cm.). Kimbell Art Museum, Fort Worth, Texas.

About Art History

Scenes depicting ritual sacrifices, bloodlettings, and other spiritual ceremonies are prevalent in Mayan relief carvings from the classic period. Because these events were of such great importance to the Maya, it is not surprising that they wanted them to be recorded and celebrated by permanent works of art such as stone carvings.

About the Artwork

This relief carving was created by a Mayan artist or stonemason in the year 785 A.D., during what is known as the classic period. The carving shows a scene in which a standing warrior presents three bound prisoners to a Mayan lord, shown seated at the upper left. Text engraved on the carving relates the story of the capture of one Mayan lord by the soldiers of another, the presentation of the captive and his companions, and the blood sacrifice of these prisoners three days later.

About the Media

This relief carving was carved from limestone found in or near the Usumacinta River valley. Traces of paint on the carving were made from minerals and plants found in the area.

About the Technique

The form of carving used in the creation of this piece is called *low relief.* Panels adorned with low-relief carvings have been found in the tombs of Mayan rulers, depicting scenes that celebrate the lives and accomplishments of these famed leaders. Various kinds of chisels and other hand tools were used to create these detailed panels. Low-relief carvings were sometimes painted with pigments that still retain much of their original vibrancy.

UNIT 2 • Lesson 5

Artist Profile

Senufo Face Mask

This mask was made by an unknown artist of the Senufo of the west African nation Ivory Coast. The Senufo were traditionally farmers. Today, there are approximately 600,000 Senufo in West Africa, and most of them live in villages of 50 to 2,000 people. They are known for their skills in woodcarving and brass casting and have been prolific in the creation of elaborate masks, such as the one featured here.

◀ **Artist unknown.** (Ivory Coast). *Senufo Face Mask.* Nineteenth to twentieth century.

Wood, horn, fiber, cloth, feather, and metal.
$14\frac{1}{2}$ inches tall (35.56 cm.).
The Metropolitan Museum of Art, New York, New York.

About Art History

Senufo artwork of all kinds is made by specialized artisans. There are several different art forms that are used to celebrate and honor Senufo ancestors, including small brass statues, miniatures, and masks. The mask shown here is an example of one of the many types of masks made by the Senufo.

About the Artwork

In Senufo culture face masks represent ancestors. The masks are worn by members of the *Poro,* a Senufo men's society, during rituals to honor and worship their ancestors. The rituals are performed at funeral services, initiation ceremonies, and during festivals where ancestors are thanked for bountiful crop harvests. This mask has a small, carved face with a smooth finish. When the mask is worn over the face, plant fibers affixed to the bottom and sides of the mask cascade down over the body of the wearer. The feathers and animal horns projecting from the sides of this mask are not a typical feature in Senufo masks and may have been added to give the mask more power to ward off evil forces threatening the community.

About the Media

This mask is made of wood, animal horns, natural plant fibers, cotton, feathers, and metal.

About the Technique

This mask appears to have been carved by hand. Fibers, feathers, and animal horns were then attached to the face portion of the wooden mask.

Artist Profile

Sleeveless Shirt (Two Cats)

It is not known who crafted this sleeveless shirt. Most likely, it was made by a skilled weaver who worked during the time of the Incas before the Spanish arrived in the mid-1500s.

◀ **Artist unknown. (Coastal Incan).** (Peru). *Sleeveless Shirt (Two Cats).* c. 1438–1532.
Wool and cotton. The Metropolitan Museum of Art, Nelson Rockefeller Collection, New York, New York.

About Art History

No written history survives to tell us about Incan textile weaving. Archaeologists and art historians can only put together the pieces they find. It is fortunate that Incan textiles were often buried in tombs and were not destroyed. Fabrics also were used as offerings to the Incan gods, and cloth has been found draped around gold statues. Textile patterns probably showed wealth and rank. Textile weaving was most likely a main source of income in Incan civilization.

About the Artwork

The images of two pumas facing each other in a mirror is used often in Incan textile art. The puma cats are standing directly across from each other. This creates symmetry. The animal figures are woven with different colored threads. Generally, Incan art used images that were simple, noble, and restrained. This is different from earlier ancient Peruvian styles, which used more complicated geometric images arranged in patterns.

About the Media

This shirt is woven with wool and cotton. Other fabrics were woven using alpaca or llama wool, and even feathers.

About the Technique

Incan textiles were hand woven by skilled artisans. The designs on the fabrics were made in a number of different ways. They were painted, stamped with a pattern, embroidered, and appliquéd.

Artist Profile

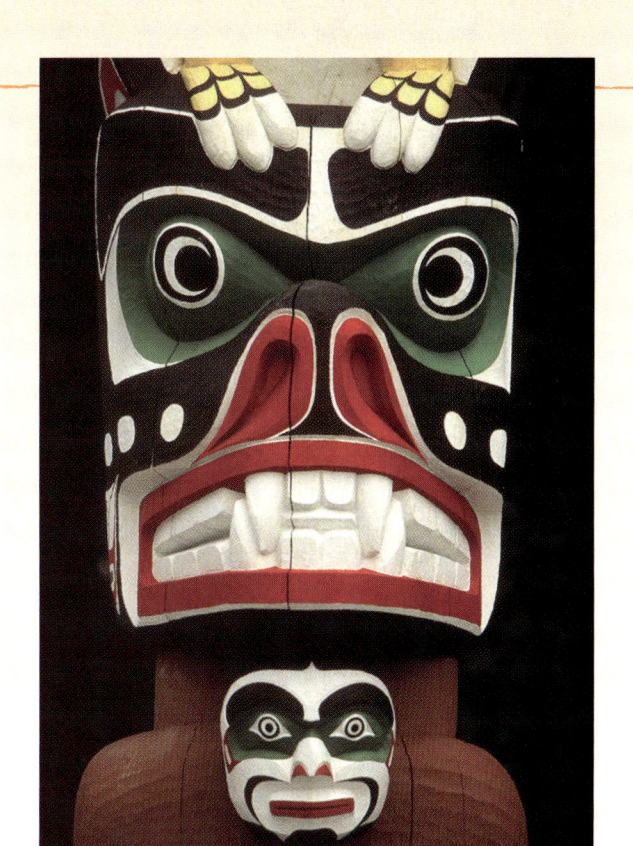

Symmetrical View of a Totem Pole

Totem poles are a traditional art form in Pacific Northwest native tribal cultures. The Kwakiutl and the Haida are two groups that made totem poles. The Kwakiutl and the Haida live in what is now the Canadian province of British Columbia. Western culture changed these native cultures by introducing Western beliefs, tools, ideas, and ways of life. The introduction of the beliefs of others greatly affected the mythology and belief systems of the Kwakiutl and Haida cultures.

◀ **Artist unknown.** (Canada). *Symmetrical View of a Totem Pole.*

Stanley Park, Vancouver, British Columbia, Canada.

About Art History

Many Pacific Northwest people built totem poles. The Haida have the most developed wood-carving skills. As Western culture took root in the Pacific Northwest, the art of totem-pole carving was almost lost. It took a great deal of effort by master carvers and the American and Canadian governments to keep the art from dying. Totem poles are still being carved in British Columbia today.

About the Artwork

This totem pole stands in Stanley Park in Vancouver, British Columbia. It depicts animals that represent traditional beliefs. The killer whale (the lord of the sea) and the wolf (the lord of the land) are linked by the frog. The raven, considered the creator god, is on top. The raven is also thought of as the source of light.

About the Media

Totem poles are carved from cedar trees, then painted and stained.

About the Technique

A totem pole is usually carved by a team that includes a master carver and apprentices. Often the carver thanks the tree for giving up its life. Once a cedar tree is cut down, the log is hollowed so it dries evenly without splitting. Carvers shape the log by cutting away the outer sapwood. The master carver draws the figure onto the tree. Carving is done with a mallet and chisel. Finally the totem pole is stained and painted. After the totem pole is finished, the people of the community eat a huge meal to celebrate.

Artist Profile

Thunderbird Shield

The Absaroke were one of the Plains cultures. They spoke the Siouan language and were called *Crow*. They lived mostly around the Yellowstone River and its territories and were a hunting culture. They were enemies of the Sioux. In battle a warrior wanted to bring as much supernatural help, or *medicine*, as possible with him. This protection was thought to be provided by the warrior's shield, facial paint, and the decorations on his garments. The shield also provided a physical defense against enemy weapons.

◀ **Artist unknown.** (United States). *Thunderbird Shield.* c. 1830.

Buffalo-hide shield with inner cover decorated with paintings and feathers. Smithsonian National Museum of the American Indian, New York, New York.

About Art History

To obtain "medicine," young men of the Plains cultures would go on a *vision quest*. For four days, a boy went off by himself and fasted. During or after this fast he might have a vision or dream. The vision often included an animal giving the boy a special power and specific rituals to make his power effective. Part of the ritual would include designing a shield.

About the Artwork

The owner of this shield believed that his personal medicine came from the thunderbird. The symbols representing the thunderbird were painted onto buffalo hide, which was then covered with feathers. The ends of some of the feathers were cut on a slant. Plains people cut feathers to symbolize cutting an enemy's throat.

About the Media

This thunderbird shield is made from buffalo hide, paint, and feathers.

About the Technique

The shield was made from stretched buffalo hide. The black, yellow, and red paints were made from powdered natural substances mixed with a glutinous substance obtained from boiling hide scrapings. The color of paint used was not common and was probably obtained through trade. The artist attached feathers to the buffalo hide.

Artist Profile

Tree of Life

Stanistawa Bakula of Poland created *Tree of Life*, but little beyond that is known about him. People learned from family members and schoolteachers how to make paper cuts. Paper cutting is a simple craft to learn, but the finished work can be intricate.

◀ **Stanistawa Bakula.** (Polish). *Tree of Life.* 1962.

Cut paper. $12\frac{3}{8} \times 7\frac{1}{2}$ inches (31 × 19 cm.).
Museum of International Folk Art, Santa Fe, New Mexico.

About Art History

Paper cutting is a tradition in Germany, China, and Japan, as well as in Poland. Polish paper cutting is called *wycinanki* (vē chē nôn kē). Paper cutting in Poland probably started in the rural farm areas sometime in the mid-nineteenth century. Social and economic factors might have allowed the peasants to use their time and resources to develop a unique paper-cutting art form. Paper cuts were used to decorate houses, furniture, and walls with bright colors. Often paper cuts were made around the Christmas and Easter holidays. Polish paper cutting was most popular at the end of the nineteenth century and the beginning of the twentieth century.

About the Artwork

This paper cut is a traditional Polish design. It looks like a silhouette because it is all black. However, many paper cuts used brilliant colors as well as black. This contrast of colors produced a surprising and vivid design. This paper cut is in the *kurpie* style. This means that it is a symmetrical design cut from a single piece of paper. The paper is folded one time and then cut with motifs, in this case, spruce trees and birds. A one-color symmetrical paper cut is called a *leluja* (le lo͞o yah).

About the Media

This *Tree of Life* is made from paper.

About the Technique

Wycinanki designs are made by folding a piece of paper, designing the image, and cutting the paper using scissors and sharp knives.

Artist Profile

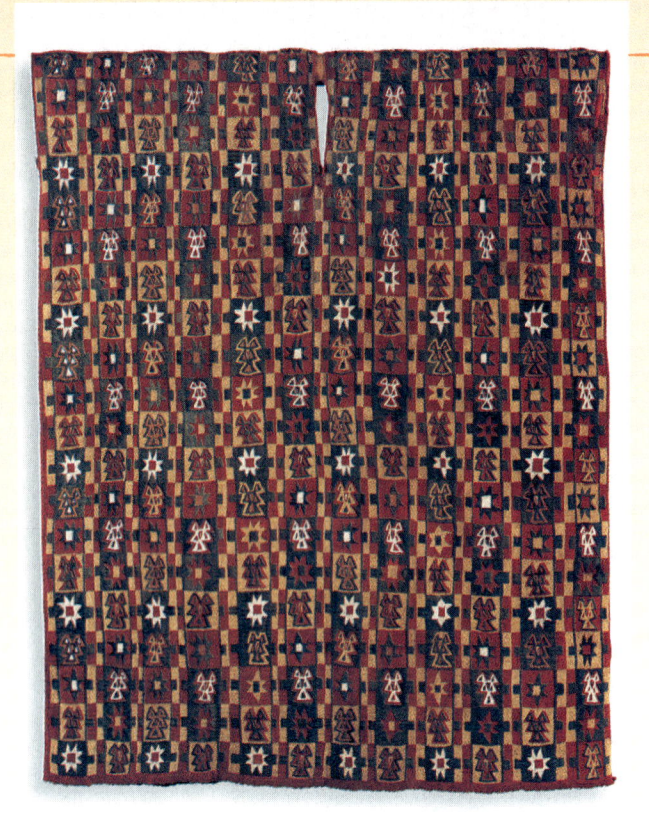

Tunic

It is not know whether this tunic was made by a particular artisan or by an ordinary Incan citizen, since cloth was designed and woven by a great many individuals in fifteenth- and sixteenth-century Peru. Taxes were imposed by Incan emperors, and a labor tax required citizens to spend a specified amount of time working for the government weaving cloth, working in the grain fields, serving in the military, or participating in public works projects, such as building roads.

◀ **Artist unknown.** (Peru). *Tunic.* 15th–16th century.
Camel hair. 37 × 29 inches (93.99 × 73.67 cm.).
The Metropolitan Museum of Art. New York, New York.

About Art History

In the sixteenth century, Spanish conquistadors conquered the Incan Empire. The conquistadors destroyed temples, homes, and other buildings, erecting their own structures in their places. They took whatever they viewed as valuable, often melting down artifacts made of precious metals and sending the silver and gold back to Spain by ship. Although textiles were of great value and importance to the Inca, they were probably not of much interest to the conquistadors and were most likely destroyed or ignored.

About the Artwork

A tunic is a long, full shirt that serves as a robe or jacket and is worn over pants or leggings. In Incan culture, richly embroidered and handsomely woven tunics, such as the one featured here, were viewed as items of tremendous value and were worn with pride as signs of prestige. Some of the finer tunics were given as gifts by the emperor to his favored subjects and military leaders. Symbols, patterns, and design motifs woven into the cloth of Incan tunics had important meanings relating to social position or military rank. This tunic features a grid pattern containing images of fish or birds and eight-pointed stars. The exact meaning or significance of these images is not known.

About the Media

Woven fiber textiles were a sign of wealth in Incan culture. Cloth, hand-loomed by individuals from dyed and carded wool, was used not only for practical purposes, such as making blankets and clothing, but was also a form of currency used to pay taxes or other debts.

About the Technique

This tunic was made from a large piece of handwoven cloth. The colorful, elaborate designs, patterns, and symbols woven into garments such as this tunic conveyed information about the wearer's social position, family background, or ethnicity.

Artist Profile

Washington's Headquarters

Washington's Headquarters was made sometime after 1876. Even though the work has no exact date, an estimate is possible because many of the images in the work have been cut out of Currier and Ives prints that were made after 1875.

▲ **Artist unknown.** (United States). *Washington's Headquarters 1780.* c. 1876.

Mixed-media. 21¼ × 28 inches (54 × 71 cm.). Smithsonian American Art Museum, Washington, D.C.

About Art History

This work was created by an unknown artist and is called *folk art*. This type of art is made by self-taught artists. Folk artists usually think of their work as a hobby rather than a profession and do it in their spare time. Currier and Ives was a firm of American lithographers founded by Nathaniel Currier in 1834. They used a new printmaking process called *lithography* that was invented in France. They printed black-and-white images, and then they hired women to hand color the prints with watercolors. Many artists became famous because Currier and Ives made their work popular.

About the Artwork

It is assumed that this work was inspired by the 100th birthday of America. The cutouts from various Currier and Ives prints have been assembled to create the narrative parts of this image. The main image of George Washington on his horse is from the print *Washington, Crossing the Delaware: on the Evening of December 25th, 1776, Previous to the Battle of Trenton* printed in 1876. The men walking downhill with a cannon are also found in that print, and the line of soldiers receding into the background is taken from *Washington Taking Command of the American Army,* also printed in 1876. The printed title at the bottom of the collage is from an undated Currier and Ives print.

About the Media

This collage is made from paper, straw, painted canvas, thread, mica, and metal. The artist has applied the straw to represent walls, hillsides, and water.

About the Technique

This artist created *Washington's Headquarters* by arranging and adhering found materials.

Artist Profile

John Sloan
1871–1951

John Sloan (jän slōn) was born in Lock Haven, Pennsylvania, in 1871. He grew up a classmate of painter William Glackens and the modern art advocate Albert C. Barnes. At the age of 16, Sloan left school to support his family. He was an avid reader and taught himself how to draw and create etchings, eventually acquiring a job as an illustrator for the *Philadelphia Inquirer* in 1892. He attended evening classes at the Pennsylvania Academy, where he became friends with Robert Henri. He soon joined Henri in an avant-garde group of young painters called The Eight, also known as the Ash Can School. Sloan exhibited with The Eight throughout his career, and although he was never able to make a living selling his paintings, his name is associated with the group's central leadership. He died in 1951 at the age of 80.

About Art History

The Eight was comprised of John Sloan and fellow artists Henri, George B. Luks, William Glackens, Everett Shinn, Arthur B. Davies, Maurice Prendergast, and Ernest Lawson. They promoted artistic independence from the then-dominant National Academy and eventually brought about a strong, independent art movement throughout the United States. Sloan and the other six group members followed Henri to New York to portray the growth and change of the multifaceted city. Although he admired his teacher, Sloan did not completely adopt Henri's style of painting. He did agree with Henri that it was important to depict subjects from the real world instead of the idealized. He worked most of his life as a newspaper and magazine illustrator and taught art classes at various schools over the years.

About the Artwork

Everyday scenes of New York's city life characterize Sloan's most prominent work. He considered himself an observer and depicted an unsentimental and expressive view of human existence. At the time Sloan painted *Hairdresser's Window,* urban planners complained that the city's rising number of billboards were threatening to overwhelm the streets of New York. Sloan addressed this issue by incorporating many artfully arranged signs in his painting that create puns about the subject matter, including "Madame Malcomb's," the name of the hair salon.

About the Media

Most of Sloan's paintings were created with oil on canvas.

About the Technique

Sloan believed it was most important to show life as it really was, which is why he did not idealize his subjects or cover up their realistic qualities.